To Professor B
Choong Soon K

Faithful Endurance

Faithful Endurance

*An Ethnography of Korean
Family Dispersal*

Choong Soon Kim

The University of Arizona Press, Tucson

THE UNIVERSITY OF ARIZONA PRESS
Copyright © 1988
The Arizona Board of Regents
All Rights Reserved

This book was set in 10/13 Linotron 202 Galliard.
Manufactured in the U.S.A.

Library of Congress Cataloging-in-Publication Data

Kim, Choong Soon, 1938–
  Faithful endurance: an ethnography of Korean family dispersal
  Choong Soon Kim.
    p. cm.

  Bibliography: p.
  Includes index.
  ISBN 0-8165-1071-7 (alk. paper)
    1. Family reunions — Korea (South)   2. Korean War, 1950–1953 —
Refugees.   3. Family — Korea (South)   I. Title.
HQ682.5.K542 1988
306.8'5'095195 — dc 19   88-20487
                                                    CIP

British Library Cataloguing in Publication data are available.

For Chŏng-a with love and gratitude

Contents

Illustrations

Tables

Preface

This book is about the tragic dispersal of Korean families as a result of the partition of the Korean peninsula after World War II in 1945 and the Korean War from 1950 to 1953. An estimated five million Koreans were sundered from their family members in those two periods and have remained separated for more than thirty years. Yet the story of their suffering and endurance is unfamiliar to the Western world. This book attempts to depict the lasting impact of war upon the lives of ordinary Koreans. It is a descriptive study of a painful situation as seen and felt by an inside participant.[1]

This book is also about the rapturous reunions of some of these families during a "reunion telethon" produced by the Korean Broadcasting System in the summer of 1983.

An earlier version of the manuscript included both an ethnography and an effort at inductive generalization from the ethnography using Francis L. K. Hsu's psychocultural attributes of the father-son dyad.[2] Perhaps, I was either too ambitious or too naive. The manuscript turned out to be too long to be an effective voice for these voiceless people. Also, I realized that a too rigidly academic analysis could easily overshadow the personal accounts of suffering and endurance. I finally decided to leave the more theoretical portion of the original manuscript for a future volume comparing Koreans with Germans, Southeast Asians, and other dispersed peoples. Thus, this book became an ethnography of the poignant histories of war-torn Korean families.

I could not have accomplished a study of this nature solely by my own will and effort. I had the aid of many people and organizations. However, since it is almost impossible to establish a hierarchy of indebtedness, I will begin by thanking my family. To my parents, I owe an intellectual and emotional debt that can never be adequately repaid. To my wife, Sang-Boon, who had to carry a heavy burden while I was away from home for fieldwork and then while I was writing this book, I am indebted the most. My two sons, John and Drew, have offered constant encouragement and support.

My gratitude is also due my mentor, Pyong Choon Hahm, who taught, advised, and encouraged me from my law school years at Yonsei University in Seoul until his tragic death in a North Korean terrorist bombing in Rangoon, Burma, on October 9, 1983, while accompanying the president of South Korea on a state visit. I wish to thank two other mentors, Francis L. K. Hsu and Wilfrid C. Bailey, for their advice. I am indebted to James L. Peacock and John Shelton Reed for their encouragement in undertaking this work. I am also indebted to Roger L. Janelli, Laurel Kendall, Clayburn L. Peeples, John H. Peterson, Jr., and Hendrick Serrie for taking time to read the early version of the manuscript and offering many invaluable suggestions. I owe many thanks to Norvel H. Cook, Roger T. Fisher, Larry C. Ingram, and Frank L. Windham, who read my manuscript in part or in whole and offered many comments. Sheila K. Sharpe typed the first draft.

Special gratitude is due the Faculty Research Grants from the University of Tennessee at Martin, which supported the fieldwork for this study. I also benefited greatly from the strong support of the Department of Sociology and Anthropology at the university. Without the permission, arrangements, and support of the Republic of Korea National Red Cross, my work could not have been done successfully.

I am grateful to the *Dong-A Ilbo* newspaper for its support and permission to use the information collected by its reporters during the reunion telethon and to reproduce their photographs; the U.S. Department of the Army for permission to reproduce photographs from *Korea—1950*; Kyoo-whan Hyun for permission to quote from *Han'guk iyumin-sa*; and Larry T. McGehee for permission to quote from his column. Vernon M. Matlock reproduced the photographs from the originals.

Another debt of gratitude is owed to my many Korean friends and relatives, especially Eun-Bum Choe, Cheol-Wha Cho, Byong-Kwan Kim, Chae-Ju Lee, Kyung-Hee Kim, and Si-Uk Nam. Without their unqualified support, my fieldwork would have been difficult. Kwan-Joong Joo, Suk-Jung Han, Sung-Chae Hong, Yong-Hee Chong, Hoe-Hwan Son, and Hyon-Suk Chang have been gracious hosts, wonderful supporters, and invaluable guides.

I am thankful to the University of Arizona Press for its enthusiastic support and expeditious evaluation, and to Stephanie M. Fowler for meticulous editing. I am also indebted to the anonymous readers consulted by the Press for their constructive criticisms that have improved this book.

I owe very special thanks to the dispersed Korean families whose accounts are included in this book for their hospitality and cooperation, without which this book could not have been written.

Choong Soon Kim
Scenic Hills, Tennessee
Summer 1987

Faithful Endurance

CHAPTER I

Korean Family Dispersal

WOUNDED REMNANTS

The fratricidal Korean War, from June 25, 1950, to July 27, 1953, resulting from the partition of the peninsula that grew out of the ideological conflict between North and South Korea, produced enormous casualties.[1] As in any war, civilian casualties outnumbered those of the military, there being one million civilian casualties and three hundred thousand military.[2] In South Korea, in addition to two hundred thirty thousand wounded, the war created some three hundred thousand widows, three hundred thirty thousand permanently handicapped, one hundred thousand orphans, and one million tuberculosis cases.[3] Precise figures for North Korean casualties are not available, but it is reasonable to assume that they would be similar to those of the south.[4]

Family dispersal stemming from the partition of the Korean peninsula along the thirty-eighth parallel and the subsequent war was devastating. Although a truce was reached and a ceasefire came into effect over thirty years ago, the wounded remnants of the war persist—the estimated five million Koreans who were sundered from their families.

Family members divided by the thirty-eighth parallel have faced not only physical separation but the virtual impossibility of communicating with one another. This lack of communication has had particularly harmful consequences for spouses who were separated. Some estranged spouses in the south, believing that their loved ones are still alive in the north, have never remarried. Others have remarried, assuming that their chances for reunion with their spouses are remote, if not impossible.

Until the highly publicized reunion telethon by the Korean Broadcasting System (KBS) was held during the summer of 1983, the problem of sundered families in Korea was unknown in the West. Even in Korea, for those aware of the tragedy, it was no longer such an immediate issue. Many Koreans born after the war are unable to comprehend the war or the misery of the war in the context of family dispersal.[5]

FIELDWORK

I have done most of my fieldwork among powerless and often-forgotten people. During 1969 and 1970 I did a study of blacks and poor white pulp-wood workers in southern Georgia communities. At the time, I was able to convince the research staff of the American Pulpwood Association Harvesting Research Project (APA-HRP) to let me collect human stories of the workers instead of less meaningful statistics. I still do not know why the APA-HRP funded a project proposed by an ethnologist like me (Miles Richardson has described an ethnologist as an "uncertain scientist"[6]) over an elaborate study, full of scientific jargon, proposed by an articulate in-dustrial psychologist.

In 1974, while working as field research director for a socioeconomic and demographic study of an Indian tribe in the American South, I was recommended for the position of chief planner for the tribe by a friend who was also a practicing anthropologist. He felt that my being an Asian who shared morphological similarities with native Americans might be an advantage in this job, and that my ethnic identity as an Asian anthro-pologist might raise an interesting methodological discussion for anthro-pological fieldwork.[7] In 1978 I worked as research director for the Indian Management Services in studying adult education for eastern Indians. I was appointed because a tribal chief who was the president of the organi-zation had come to like and trust me while I was working for his tribe in 1974.[8]

The project to account for dispersed Korean family members came into being somewhat incidentally. Like most Koreans of my generation, I had participated in the Korean War. I had felt it in my very bones, witnessing the carnage with my own young eyes. Many people lost their loved ones forever, and many others were separated from their family members. Yet the idea of documenting this tragic saga of family separation had never occurred to me during my stay in America of nearly two decades.

After leaving Korea in 1965, I had no opportunity to return for even a brief visit until the summer of 1981, when the Institute of Foreign Affairs and National Security, Ministry of Foreign Affairs of South Korea, invited me to conduct seminars on American culture for three months. Although both of my parents had passed away during my absence from Korea, my siblings had not notified me until their funerals were over. Perhaps they thought I could not have done anything anyway, even if I could have afforded to come. But being excluded from my parents' funerals made me feel even more physically and emotionally isolated from my homeland, residing in what I felt (and still feel) to be an alien land. I felt as if I were walking a tightrope between two cultures, not fully a part of either. I had achieved "the sense of distancing from self," my Korean self, if I may borrow the words of James W. Fernandez.[9]

During that first return to Korea (emotionally my feeling was of "going," not "returning"), as I was kneeling at the graves of my parents, I thought of the hundreds and thousands of fellow Koreans who had been sundered from their family members in the north. I took comfort in the knowledge that my parents were no longer in this world and witnesses to the sad realities of Korea's plight. And most northern refugees were not as fortunate as I was, for they did not know whether their loved ones were living or dead. This visit to Korea inspired my determination to return to document the sorrows of dispersed families there.

After having been gone so long, I was overwhelmed by the apparent cultural upheaval in South Korea. Experiencing so suddenly the results of years of modernization and Westernization, I felt as though struck with a case of "future shock." I cannot find the words for the exact feelings I had —the feelings of a stranger in a familiar land. I felt strange, uncertain, and insecure for the more than two months of my first return to Korea. And I was told later by my relatives and friends that they had had an uneasy feeling toward me—I had a familiar face but a stranger's feel.

Occasionally I was frustrated by my inability to grasp the changes that had taken place during my absence. Sometimes I found myself searching for the things that I had romanticized in my mind for so many years while I was living in an alien land. But most of the old, traditional ways had been altered. My "Korean self" and knowledge about Korean culture were from the Korea of 1965, and I was unable to adjust to the new Korea that I saw. In fact, Korea had experienced more drastic change during the period of my absence, from 1965 to 1981, than at any other time in its modern history. Thus, there was a cultural vacuum in my mind.

Despite my efforts, in the early days of my reentry to Korea, I found it very difficult, if not impossible, to feel comfortable or have a feeling of "oneness" with native Koreans. I had anticipated that I would not be as comfortable as I had been during my first fieldwork there, from 1963 to 1964. Then, as a research associate in the Social Science Research Institute at Yonsei University, I had participated in a project supported by an Asian Foundation grant to study the compatibility of traditional Korean customs with the modern legal system. I was one member of a four-person research team that collected data. Because of my interest, and being the only single person among the four, I spent almost a year in different Korean villages, moving from place to place by every available mode of transportation—by plane, train, bus, taxi, bike, but primarily by foot. Although I was not fully trained in anthropological field methods, I felt confident working with other Koreans. However, when I went back in 1982, as a trained anthropologist who had conducted fieldwork in the United States, I found that I had become cautious, hesitant, and even reluctant about doing fieldwork in Korea. This might have been a result of my fieldwork in other cultures and a process of becoming "reflexive."[10]

Not only was I having to cope with the anguish of a person reentering his native land, I was having the problem of dealing with an atypical setting for anthropological fieldwork. The size of the target population was enormous—in the millions—and the extent of the field was the entire Korean peninsula. Even if this study was to be descriptive, selecting representative informants would be important.[11] Dispersed family members were not residing within a single community or town but were widely scattered. Had they made up their own compact community, it would have been much easier for me to conduct intensive fieldwork.

Coincidentally, in the summer of 1983, after I had almost completed my interviews and collecting background material, the Korean Broadcasting System (KBS) introduced the reunion telethon. KBS literally created a village of the dispersed as hundreds and thousands of Koreans gathered in Yŏido Square (later named Reunion Plaza) in downtown Seoul to register for the telethon. One could not have created such a field setting for an anthropologist even with unlimited research funds. It was ideal for intensive fieldwork and an unexpected bonanza for me.

My field methods included interviewing informants, gathering documents, collecting life histories (also known to others as biographies or personal documents),[12] and participant observation. Without participant observation, my attempts to eliminate my earlier feelings of insecurity and uncertainty and of being a stranger would have been difficult, perhaps unsuccessful. This participant observation included a tour to the truce village of P'anmunjŏm in the demilitarized zone (DMZ) in the summer of 1982. South Korean citizens are generally not permitted to visit P'anmunjŏm.[13]

In P'anmunjŏm I felt chilled witnessing the confrontation between the North Korean soldiers and the United Nations forces, facing each other along the border. The North Korean soldiers' uniforms brought back long-forgotten memories of the Korean War. It was the same uniform that had frightened me when a North Korean soldier pointed his loaded gun at my father to banish us from our country estate during the north's invasion of the south in the summer of 1950.

I also toured the "invasion tunnel" discovered in November 1974 by the South Koreans. It had been dug by the North Koreans as a possible means of invading the south. Two caged canaries were at the last stopping point to the north. As American mine workers used birds to check for poisonous gas, the South Korean military also used them to detect possible leaks of poisonous gas from the northern end of the tunnel. These two small birds symbolize the unfortunate reality of the partition of the peninsula. On the way back from the tour, I found it hard to speak to anyone and kept to myself. Forgotten memories of the war crept into my mind. I cannot, after all, erase the fact that I too am a "child of war." [14]

From my preliminary fieldwork in the summer of 1982, I gained some general knowledge about sundered families in South Korea. I did not know the subject was so politically sensitive, however, until I returned to Korea in the winter of 1982 to continue my project. Occasionally, the North Korean authorities would train as espionage agents South Koreans who had either fled or who had been kidnapped to the north, sending them back south to make contact with their relatives. According to current South Korean anticommunist law, if one of these spies contacts a South Korean citizen, even if the citizen is a parent, sibling, or other close kin of the presumed agent, the South Korean is committing a crime if such contact is not reported to the police. The South Korean Central Intelligence Agency (KCIA) is one of the undercover agencies that detect such espionage activities. At the North-South Korean Red Cross talks in 1971, the third-ranking South Korean delegate was an officer of the KCIA.

Further evidence of the strict enforcement of anticommunist rules is the fact that until June 23, 1973, when former South Korean president

Chung-hee Park announced his foreign policy for peaceful reunification, any South Korean whose dispersed family members were in North Korea —even if they had been kidnapped by the North Koreans—was carefully screened before, if not prohibited from, traveling overseas. I realized that my informants must be able to trust me.

In spite of the publicity generated by the telethon, people were still reluctant to answer questions, and sensitive responses from the dispersed members were noticeable. One day in the summer of 1983, while helping volunteers from the Republic of Korea National Red Cross (hereinafter referred to as the South Korean Red Cross) register applicants for their television appearances, I was introduced to sixty-year-old Chong-wŏn Hahm, who was registering for the reunion telethon to search for his former wife. He had been separated from her in early December 1950 in Hŭngnam, North Korea, when the United Nations and the South Korean forces were retreating from occupied North Korea. Leaving his wife in the north, he had fled south alone. Later he remarried in the south and had a son and a daughter.

Chong-wŏn insisted that he fill out the application form by himself, but I offered him my assistance because I wanted to talk to him. As my questioning intensified, Chong-wŏn became disturbed by my interview. Showing his identification card, he screamed at me, "I am not a communist. I have been a good citizen. Why do you ask me about my past as if I was a communist or communist sympathizer?" He thought I was an undercover agent, even though I was wearing a Red Cross badge like the other Red Cross workers. I was embarrassed by the scene as people who were waiting in line to register stared at us and began to look as if they were ready to assault me. A Red Cross official took me to a safe place until the commotion was over. I felt that in this incident I had barely avoided a dangerous situation that could have become much worse.

Considering the sensitivity of my study, I attempted to select representative informants who could tell me their detailed life histories. I wanted informants that would typify different social positions in the Korean family, that is, as parent, spouse, or child. Furthermore, I sought informants from various socioeconomic levels of Korean society. In addition, my informants had to be trustworthy and free from suspicion of me. I decided to select them from among my relatives, close friends, and close friends of my friends.[15] My relationship to each informant is explained in the case studies.

I selected five individuals for case studies. One was an elderly woman longing for the son she had been separated from during World War II. She would represent the anguish of Korean mothers sundered from their children and also portray the saga of Korean dispersal that began even before the partitioning of the country in 1945. I also chose a South Korean woman, a North Korean woman, and a North Korean man, all of whom had remained single after being separated from their spouses, to depict the pain of many sundered couples. My fifth case had been separated as a child from his parents in 1948. His story would reveal the agony of many now middle-aged North Korean refugees who still yearn for their parents.

Selecting key informants from among relatives and friends not only minimized their possible suspicions of me as a spy but also reduced the likelihood of their misinforming me. This is not to say that Koreans do not lie to their relatives and friends. They often do. According to Clark W. Sorensen's analysis, however, misinformation from Korean informants has been limited largely to certain situations.[16] Probable deceptions were easier to verify than among strangers by my being able to cross-check with other relatives and mutual friends.[17]

There is no way to judge if the people I selected as case studies for this book are representative of all dispersed family members in Korea. The exact number of Koreans separated from their families before, during, and after the Korean War is unknown. Nevertheless, I am confident that any mother who has been separated from her children will share the feelings I delineate in this book. So also will the dispersed spouses and the children torn from their parents. I hope many of them can claim that I have also told their stories.

I personally gathered the life histories of the five people I selected. The circumstances under which the interviews were conducted are discussed in each account. I had learned much about one of my informants before I interviewed him. The life history of the North Korean who had been dispersed from his wife and who had remained single after moving to the south, had been published in a daily newspaper. The paper ran installments of his story for several months, and later these were published as a single volume. However, upon his request, I did not cite his autobiography as a reference. Since my interviews included some information not told in his published autobiography, I made an effort to conceal his identity.

I have also incorporated several accounts of family members reunited during the 1983 telethon by the use of various media—television, newspaper, computer, and wall poster. These accounts are based on my field notes taken during the telethon and on written reports that appeared in newspapers and magazines.

Additional information on each of the reunited families was collected by seven reporters on special assignment from the *Dong-A Ilbo* (one of the oldest and most prestigious daily newspapers in Korea). Under an arrangement with the *Dong-A Ilbo*, I have used the information collected by those reporters for my work. (Parenthetically, while attending a lunch- eon meeting with executives of the *Dong-A Ilbo* during the summer of 1983 [the time of the telethon], I had initially suggested gathering such infor- mation, including photographs, for a future publication to be written in Korean.) Their efforts were indispensable for this project. Without them, I would have been unable to document many detailed accounts. At the time, it would have been impossible for me to trace any of the thousands of reunited families because I was working at the registration desk. More- over, the newspaper reporters had access to the KBS studio, which I was not allowed to have. The reporters who collected the information were not trained in anthropology, but their accounts were vivid, and I could not have done better.[18]

The range of my interviews was not limited to those whose stories are told in this book but also included members of many other dispersed fami- lies, Korean politicians and political insiders, intellectuals and scholars, and laymen and officials who have taken a vital part in the North-South Red Cross talks on family reunion. I also collected vast quantities of historical and contemporary documents, including articles in the daily press and in weekly and monthly journals, stylistically ranging from crass sensational- ism to thoughtful discussion.

THEORETICAL ORIENTATION AND METHODOLOGY

My orientation in anthropology is toward "humanistic insight com- bined with the critical and detached and generalizing methods of science," emulating the work of Robert Redfield, who was my mentor's mentor.[19] My commitment can be reiterated by quoting the elegant words of Red- field: "With half his being the social scientist approaches his subject matter with a detachment he shares with the physicist. With the other half he approaches it with a human sympathy which he shares with the novelist."[20] According to Redfield, the success of some epochmaking works, such as Tocqueville's *Democracy in America*, Sumner's *Folkways*, and Veblen's *The Theory of the Leisure Class*,[21] is largely due to the fact that such works are "an expression of some perception of human nature," and "each brings forward significant generalizations."[22]

Generalizations are not brought forward in this book. According to James W. Fernandez, however, the works of Bronislaw Malinowski, Ruth Benedict, E. E. Evans-Pritchard, Marcel Griaule, and Clyde Kluckhohn, for instance, are considered "major 'points de repère' in anthropology" not because of their theoretical contributions but because of their "skillful presentation of local point of view."[23] Fernandez relates that "they did not allow that essential academic interest to override local realities."[24] I too want to be an ethnographer first and ethnologist second.

In undertaking fieldwork for this project, I have not employed any specific theory other than a humanistic approach with sympathetic understanding. My nonalliance with a particular theory is not because I consider existing theories inchoate.[25] I simply do not belong to any particular school of anthropological thought.

Methodologically, a growing number of anthropologists have engaged in research in their own societies.[26] Such work has many labels: "insider anthropology," "native anthropology," and "indigenous anthropology," to name a few.[27] Methodological discussions of such studies have flourished. My fieldwork has, to a certain extent, an additional dimension. Unlike most native anthropologists who have initially done fieldwork in an alien culture, I began with fieldwork at home, continued with alien cultures, and then returned home for further fieldwork.

Fieldwork in one's own society has the advantage of allowing one to develop more insight into the native culture and to arrive at abstractions from the native's point of view. Practically speaking, it is economical in that it does not require travel to remote places, and it takes less time—one need not learn a foreign language and become acquainted with alien customs.[28] Such arguments are all familiar and well documented in anthropological literature.

There are times, however, when being a non-native is an advantage in studying a culture and being a native doing research in one's own society is disadvantageous. When I was in the field in the American South, many people, recognizing that I was a foreigner who needed help, would insist

on taking me to my destination when I asked directions. They would carefully pronounce or even spell words when answering my questions. I was
unable to enjoy such advantages in working at home. My first fieldwork
in Korea in 1963 suffered from the traditional Korean custom whereby
females are to avoid strange men. When I was allowed to talk to a young
woman, her parents would hang a curtain between us, and an elder family
member would always be present. Since I was a Korean, the native villagers
being studied expected me to conform to their norms because I belonged
to the same culture.[29] If I had been a foreigner, customs would not have
been strictly followed. Hortense Powdermaker had more difficulties in
crossing the racial boundary during her fieldwork in a rural Mississippi
community than I had in a similar community there during fieldwork.[30]
Myrna Sayles also relates such difficulties.[31]

The major critics of anthropological work at home, according to the
assessment of John L. Aguilar, "have characterized such knowledge as
mere subjective involvement, a deterrent to objective perception and analysis."[32] Nonetheless, the inherent bias of being an anthropologist doing
work among the natives of one's own country[33] can be reduced, if not
eliminated, by studying other cultures before studying one's own and by
"distancing" oneself from the natives both physically and psychologically.[34]
For instance, Emiko Ohnuki-Tierney, a native Japanese who has studied
her own people in Kobe, Japan, and who has also conducted fieldwork in
an alien culture (Sakhalin Ainu who were relocated to Hokkaido in 1945),
offers very meaningful discussions of methodology.[35] Her effort to be reflexive in her fieldwork in her native home with her own people has basically been accomplished by achieving "the sense of distancing from self,"
as James W. Fernandez has suggested.[36] To help "distance" herself physically and psychologically from the natives being studied, to prevent too
much immersion in her native culture, and to regain a sense of reflective
perspective as an anthropologist, Ohnuki-Tierney reduced the duration of
her fieldwork from six months to four. She also alluded to the value of
studying another culture before undertaking the study of one's own.[37] The
benefits of studying other cultures before studying one's own are widely
appreciated by seasoned fieldworkers, even by talented veterans such as
M. N. Srinivas.[38] Donald A. Messerschmidt reports, "Some social research
firms hiring anthropologists to study American society these days still feel
that research in another society is an important precondition to successful
research in one's own."[39]

I have attempted to develop the needed reflexivity and the ability to look at Koreans and their culture objectively. I feel I have been successful to a certain extent. I had the feeling of being a stranger in Korea when I first returned there. In an effort to maintain distancing, I did not stay any longer than three months on any of my four field trips (summer 1982, winter 1982, summer 1983, and winter 1984). Both winters trips were less than one month. I have to confess, however, that except for the first two months of my first return to Korea from America in the summer of 1981, I became readily reenculturated and immersed in Korean life. I discovered that maintaining my detachment was more easily said than done. Once I had reestablished rapport with my own people, distancing myself from them was doubly hard.

Perhaps our anthropological community has polarized the roles of insider (native) and outsider (non-native). I believe one can overcome the weaknesses of being either an insider or an outsider by being aware of the shortcomings of each vantage point and by making a conscientious effort. Some talented insiders can distance themselves in their studies of their own people, and many perceptive outsiders can understand the "innards" of alien cultures. When I had completed the first draft of this book, an astute American anthropologist and folklorist who has done fieldwork in Korea and published a major book about Korea pointed out a mistake I had made in describing a clan name. It should have been P'ungsan Yu, not Munhwa Yu. I made this error even though one of my sisters is married to a member of the P'ungsan Yu clan and still lives in the village of the clan. Outsiders can often be more perceptive in some ways than insiders.

Whether I have been successful or not, my determination to be detached from my Korean self was so pronounced in my mind that I was unable to take full advantage of being an insider. I had made myself a marginal fieldworker, neither insider nor outsider. My role was blurred. This was also true regarding my roles as ethnographer and as informant. I could have been an excellent informant for my project. Lawrence Hennigh demonstrated that as an anthropologist he could also be a good informant in his study of a town in rural Oregon.[40] Although my emphasis on "distancing" weakened my own role as a key informant despite my professional training, I believe that it is possible for a practicing anthropologist to be a trustworthy informant.

My experience during this study also showed me that, whatever effort one makes, as long as one is involved in studying one's own society, some subjectivity is inescapable. But as M. N. Srinivas has indicated, "the very awareness of subjectivity" can be a step toward achieving greater objectivity.[41]

ETHICS, ROMANIZATION, AND SCOPE

Adhering to the ethics of my discipline, I have tried to protect the privacy and uphold the dignity of the individuals who are presented in this book. I have employed pseudonyms for individuals, clans, and locations, even when an individual's identity, clan, and location name have been widely publicized in the Korean media, for I do not want this to be used as a source book for identifying the individuals or other written documents that contain their names. I have done so even though Korean custom considers using a pseudonym an intolerable personal insult. Koreans often use the expression "I will change my family name if that is not true," much as Americans might say "I swear that is true." Nevertheless, I have chosen to put the protection of individual privacy before the violation of Korean mores.[42] I have been relieved to learn, however, that American colleagues who have adopted this practice in their anthropological work have not received any negative response from Koreans.

In this book Korean terms, including the names of persons and localities, are romanized according to the McCune-Reischauer system. The exceptions are the few Koreans who have established different romanizations for their names. Contrary to Korean (and Japanese) usage, I give the family names of people last, except in the bibliography, where Korean and Japanese authors are listed by their family names followed by a comma before their personal names.

My observing and interviewing were limited to South Korea because I was unable to go to North Korea. Even in collecting documents, my efforts were confined to the south. Except for some less reliable secondary sources and piecemeal information, I was not able to consult any thoughtful anthropological scholarship on fieldwork in North Korea.[43] Because of such limitations, this work cannot treat both Koreas equally. If one day I gain access to the north, I may have an opportunity to correct this imbalance. In the meantime, I have made every effort to avoid misleading readers, making unsupported assumptions about North Korea, or presenting a distorted image of North Korean society.

The official name of South Korea is the Republic of Korea (ROK) and of North Korea, the Democratic People's Republic of Korea (DPRK). Throughout this book, however, the informal designations North Korea and South Korea are adopted for easier reading, implying neither a positive or negative connotation. I do not want to undermine or discredit the integrity of either regime.

The focus of this book is on family dispersal that occurred during the Korean War, but previous dispersal of Korean families is also discussed. Chapter 2 describes this earlier sundering, which began prior to the liberation of Korea from Japan in 1945 and continued until the Korean War.

To assist readers in understanding Korean family life in the context of the Korean family and kinship system, a brief description of that system is included in Chapter 3.

Chapter 4 is the life history of an elderly woman who was separated from her son during World War II. Chapter 5 contains the accounts of three Koreans who have remained single since being severed from their spouses during the Korean War. Chapter 6 is an account of a North Korean man who fled to the south in his boyhood, leaving his parents in the north.

Chapter 7 summarizes reunion efforts of the Red Cross and other organizations, the press, and the South Korean government. The emotional reunions of the families brought together by newspapers, computer matches, and the highly publicized reunion telethon are also portrayed. Chapter 8 describes four separated families and recounts how their reunions were brought about: by the telethon, by a list of reunion applicants published in a special edition of a newspaper, by wall posters displayed in the Reunion Plaza, and by a computerized identification system installed at the national police headquarters. Finally, in Chapter 9, some personal remarks as an anthropologist are related.

Because I wanted to make this book accessible to a rather diverse audience, I have tried to minimize disciplinary terminology but maximize usage of footnotes, thereby enabling interested readers to pursue the subject in more depth than can be provided in a single volume.

CHAPTER 2

Historical Background

Chosŏn, the Korean version of the Chinese phrase *chao-hsien,* may be roughly translated "morning calm and freshness." From this, Korea acquired the epithet by which it is still known today, "the land of the morning calm." Those familiar with its geopolitical history, however, may wonder if Korea has ever been calm. Instead of tranquility, historical evidence indicates that Koreans have often been awakened to the clattering of horses' hooves or the artillery fire of foreign intruders. The peninsula has seemingly been "the land of broken calm," as the subtitle of Shannon McCune's book on Korea indicates.[1]

Geographically, Korea is in the middle of the Far East. The long northern border of the Korean peninsula is linked with the vast expanse of Manchuria, an area almost forty-three times Korea's size. Comparison of Korea with the Russo-Siberian land mass, with which it shares an eleven-mile border, is almost beyond comprehension. Across the Sea of Japan (or the East Sea, as Koreans prefer to call it) sits the island nation of Japan, almost 70 percent larger than Korea. The channel between these two nations is so narrow that on a clear day Tsushima Island of Japan can be seen from Pusan on the southeastern tip of Korea.

As a consequence, the peninsula has always been vulnerable to attacks from neighboring states. In addition to invasion and domination by Chinese dynasties over the centuries,[2] there have been continual intrusions

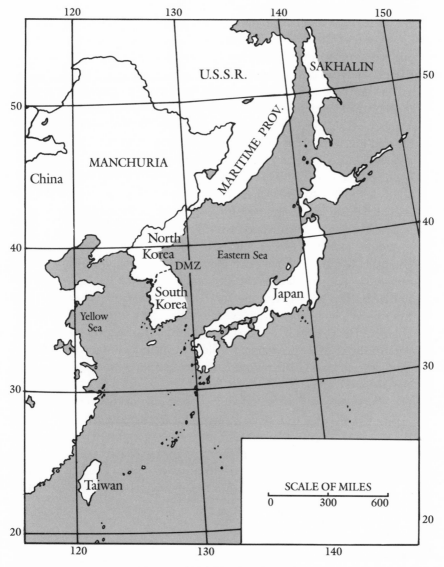

120	130	140	150

U.S.S.R.

SAKHALIN

50

50

MANCHURIA

China

MARITIME PROV.

40

40

North
Korea

DMZ

Eastern Sea

South
Korea

Japan

Yellow
Sea

30

30

20

SCALE OF MILES

0   300   600

20

| 120 | 130 | 140 |

Taiwan

Korea and Neighboring Countries

from nomadic northern tribes such as the Yen, Khitan, Jurchen, and Mongol.[3] The rise and fall of Chinese dynasties has had a profound impact on the security of the country. Furthermore, two full-scale Japanese invasions into Korea by Toyotomi Hideyoshi in the sixteenth century devastated the Korean Yi dynasty.[4]

Koreans have long been acutely aware of the foreign threat posed to them by their geopolitical situation. Taewŏn'gun of the Yi dynasty adopted a policy of isolationism in direct response to Western incursion, but in the mid-nineteenth century Japan, China, Russia, some European nations, and the United States pressured Korea to open its doors to outsiders in the name of modernization. Competing foreigners clashed on Korean soil, which led to the Russo-Japanese War of 1904–1905. Victory in this conflict provided Japan with a firm base for sole control of the peninsula, which it annexed in 1910 and maintained as a colony until 1945.

Despite persistent foreign threats, invasions, and incursions, the Korean peninsula had been united since the seventh century; except in rare and temporary instances, it had remained undivided, protected on its northern border by two great rivers, the Yalu and the Tumen.[5] Even when Korea lost its sovereignty under Japanese colonial rule, it was still ruled as a single country. The peninsula was first divided in 1945, along the thirty-eighth parallel, by the foreign-imposed Cold War. Although the entire population suffered during the period of Japanese colonization and then from the division of their country after World War II, Koreans were to experience far worse—the worst suffering of their long history. This time their agony was not due to foreign intruders or interference but to a fratricidal war. The Korean War lasted from 1950 to 1953, and in 1953 the dividing line was modified and maintained by the establishment of the DMZ. These historical ordeals created the dispersal of Korean families. Members of Korean families are scattered throughout neighboring countries and are still divided by the DMZ.

KOREANS IN CHINA

The Korean influx into China has occurred throughout its history because of its geographic proximity. Many Koreans were taken to China as captives during invasions of the T'ang, Yüan, and Ch'ing dynasties between the seventh and nineteenth centuries. Since the beginning of the Yi dynasty in 1392, many Koreans have emigrated to Manchuria to seek farmland. In 1864 and 1869 many Koreans crossed the Manchurian border to escape severe droughts that plagued the peninsula. By 1907, for example, the Korean population in Chientao, Manchuria, across the Yalu and Tumen rivers, had reached 71,000.[6]

The growth of the Korean population in Manchuria increased drastically with the threat of Japanese annexation. When annexation seemed inevitable, it was estimated that approximately 10,000 Koreans began moving to Chientao annually. In 1910, the year Japan annexed Korea, a great many political refugees crossed the Manchurian border seeking asylum. That year the Korean population in Chientao reached 109,500.[7] Not only did China provide sanctuary for Koreans wanting to escape Japanese rule, it provided a base for Korean anti-Japanese independence fighters. Moreover, China allowed Koreans to establish a provisional government in Shanghai and permitted Korean leaders of the anti-Japanese movement to come to that city. In addition, many Chinese protected and hid Korean escapees from the Japanese army, who had been drafted by the Japanese and sent to the China front. In Chientao Korean independence fighters established military bases from which to engage Japan in armed conflict.

When Japanese colonial efforts intensified, a large number of Koreans participated in a nationwide anti-Japanese demonstration on March 1, 1919, declaring Korean independence from Japan: it became known as *samil undong,* or "the March First Movement." Many of the survivors of the movement who escaped Japanese retaliatory measures fled abroad, mainly to Manchuria. By the end of 1919 the Korean population in all of Manchuria had greatly increased, to 314,709.[8]

Beginning in the late 1920s, Koreans also moved to Manchuria to work voluntarily for the Japanese. By 1929 there were 382,405 Koreans living there. This figure began to increase radically after the Japanese established Manchukuo in 1932. When World War II ended, about 2 million Koreans were in Manchuria.[9] When it was liberated from Japan, an estimated 800,000 Koreans returned home, but about 1.2 million elected to remain in Manchuria.[10] Almost 1.8 million Koreans still reside in China, the country with the largest Korean population outside the Korean peninsula.[11]

Those Koreans who chose to continue to live in Manchuria anticipated that they would be able to visit or write their relatives and friends in Korea as they pleased, because Korea had been liberated from Japan. But at the end of World War II their homeland was divided, with the pro-Russian communist regime in the north and the pro-American regime in the south divided along the thirty-eighth parallel, and any movement of Koreans from Manchuria to South Korea was completely cut off by this partition. At the same time, the Koreans in China found that their host country was undergoing radical change. In October 1949 the communist state of the People's Republic of China was established.

The relationship between the People's Republic of China and South Korea was adversarial during the Cold War era. In 1950, when it sent its volunteer army into the Korean War to assist its communist neighbor, China became South Korea's enemy. Since that time, there has been virtually no contact between the two nations, and until the 1970s, Korean residents in Manchuria were unable to communicate with their family members and friends in South Korea.[12]

The scarcity of scientific, scholarly, and analytical work on Koreans in Manchuria does not allow me to depict accurately their life there. However, since the Nixon administration, when relations between the United States and the People's Republic of China were improved, the flow of information about Koreans in Manchuria has increased. Several naturalized American citizens of Korean ancestry have been permitted to visit their families and friends in Manchuria, and some of them have been able to invite their relatives to the United States. The limited information available from visitors and exchange scholars indicates that Koreans in China are legally Chinese citizens, quite unlike the position of Koreans in Japan. The Chinese apparently have mounted no systematic and institutionalized discrimination against Koreans on the basis of their national origin.[13] The basic policy of the People's Republic of China toward various minorities seems to be one of encouraging them to preserve their ethnic heritage, a policy clearly outlined in a lecture by Xiaotong Fei in Denver, Colorado, on March 21, 1980.[14]

Most Koreans in Manchuria live gregariously, centered in the Yanbian Korean Autonomous Prefecture of Jilin province, which was established on September 3, 1952, under a policy that promoted the retention by minorities of their ethnic and cultural heritages. They are bilingual, using both the Chinese and Korean languages.[15] Koreans sustain their cultural heritage in a variety of ways. Many wear traditional Korean dress and costumes on national holidays.[16] They prefer to eat Korean food and wear Korean clothes, and they tend to marry among themselves. They think of themselves, however, as Chinese of Korean ancestry.[17] There are universities and junior colleges for Koreans in China, including a medical university, as well as many elementary schools and middle schools.[18] Students in these schools use both languages, Chinese and Korean. In 1982 a Korean museum was opened, displaying mostly relics from the struggle against the Japanese by the Korean independence fighters of Jilin province. A Korean Christian church with five hundred members was founded sixty years ago.[19] The radio and television facilities of Yanbian Broadcasting use both the Korean and Chinese languages. The *Yanbian Daily* newspaper is also bilingual.[20]

Koreans in Manchuria today seem to be less concerned with the ideological conflicts of their homeland than the preceding generation. They listen to South Korean radio and television programs and are even familiar with the popular songs of South Korea. They are generally well informed about what is going on in that nation. They tend to perceive both North and South Korea as their homelands. Whatever their perceptions of the two Koreas, however, political realities do make a difference: a Korean-Chinese may visit a close relative in the north and return safely,[21] but such casual visits to South Korea are not allowed.[22]

Letter writing between relatives in China and South Korea has been increasing, fostered by the thawing in Sino-American relations. In 1972, 42 letters from Koreans in Manchuria were sent via Japan and Hong Kong to their family members living in South Korea.[23] Then, in September 1974, the South Korean government lifted its ban forbidding its citizens to communicate with anyone living in communist countries and began allowing them to get in touch with relatives in the Soviet Union, Eastern Europe, Cuba, Mongolia, and the People's Republic of China; North Korea, however, was not included.[24] This change in policy brought 650 letters dispatched from Koreans in Manchuria; 520 of them were delivered to the addressed persons in South Korea. The remainder were undelivered because the correspondents used incorrect addresses, some of which were over thirty years old. Since then, the number of letters from Manchuria to South Korea has increased greatly. Almost 1,000 letters are now being delivered monthly.[25]

Even more noteworthy is the possibility of visits among separated relatives. As a result of efforts by the South Korean Red Cross to satisfy China's visitation requirements, sixty-one-year-old Su-yong Ahn and his wife were allowed to visit his brother in South Korea on May 22, 1982. This was the first time the People's Republic of China had issued both exit and reentry visas to Koreans in Manchuria, enabling them to visit South Korea.[26] Encouraged by the case of Su-yong Ahn and his wife, South Koreans have filed another 500 invitations to relatives in Manchuria with the South Korean Red Cross.[27] Since late 1978 a total of 189 Korean resi-

*A Japanese officer issuing mobilization slips to Koreans
drafted as laborers. Courtesy of* Dong-A Ilbo.

dents from China, mostly from Manchuria, have traveled to South Korea
to meet their relatives. Of the 189 visitors, 100 have resettled in South
Korea; the remainder returned to Manchuria. Although some Korean-
Americans have visited their relatives living in Jilin and other parts of
China, Koreans with Republic of Korea passports have thus far not been
allowed to enter China for family reunions.[28]

Athletics seem to be contributing to increased contact between China
and South Korea. In February 1983 the South Korean tennis team obtained
an official entry visa from the People's Republic of China. On April 5, 1984,
thirty members of the Chinese basketball team arrived in Seoul. Then on
April 7, 1984, four South Korean soccer team officials obtained an offi-

cial entry visa from China to discuss Asian soccer games. During the 1986 Asian Games in Seoul, 125 Chinese athletes were welcomed.

In August 1983 the People's Republic of China issued an entry visa to some South Korean government officials who wished to attend an international meeting that was to take place in China.

On March 23, 1984, Premier Zhao Ziyang of the People's Republic of China announced during a two-hour meeting with visiting Prime Minister Yasuhiro Nakasone of Japan that China would allow South Koreans to enter Chinese territory for family reunions. Also, Korean-Chinese would be permitted to visit their family members in South Korea if they wished.[29] In response, Ch'ang-sun Yu, president of the South Korean Red Cross, immediately proposed a Red Cross meeting with China to arrange visits by separated Korean families whose members were living in both countries.[30] Despite such positive gestures, it is still too early to be optimistic about future developments.

KOREANS IN JAPAN

Archaeological and linguistic evidence is inconclusive about whether or not present-day inhabitants of the Korean peninsula and the Japanese islands share a common ancestral stock.[31] The intermittent contact between the people of Korea and Japan throughout history may have altered the composition of the Japanese population. Early Korean immigrants to Japan, voluntary and involuntary, including captives taken during the Hideyoshi invasions, became so immersed in Japanese society and assimilated into Japanese culture that their Korean identities would be impossible to trace.

A massive Korean influx into Japan occurred after the Japanese annexation of Korea in 1910.[32] In a strict sense, however, these people were not dispersed Koreans, for most family members went to Japan together. A large-scale dispersal of Korean family members occurred when Japan proclaimed the National Manpower Mobilization Act in 1939. Under this act Korean laborers and military draftees were involuntarily brought to Japan to fill the manpower shortage created by the expansion of the war to Southeast Asia. The mobilized laborers were forced to work in munitions plants and coal mines and to perform various other forms of physical labor to support the war. Japan also began to recruit volunteer soldiers among the Koreans.

As Japan escalated its war effort, the National General Mobilization Law entrapped increasing numbers of Koreans. Following the Japanese attack on Pearl Harbor on December 7, 1941, Koreans became subject to the Japanese military draft in 1942. The number of Koreans drafted into the Japanese military totaled 364,186 by the end of World War II.[33] These conscripted soldiers were sent to the South Pacific, Southeast Asia, and China. Almost half of them, some 150,000, are known to have been killed or were missing in action.[34] The aggregate number of Koreans mobilized throughout the war by the Japanese government in both Korea and Japan reached almost 6 million.[35]

Of the mobilized workers, some 724,915 Koreans were sent to Japan, Sakhalin (formerly Russian), and Southeast Asia.[36] The Korean resident association in Japan, Mindan, informed the military government in Korea after the war that there were about 2.4 million Koreans in Japan.[37]

The mobilization included females ranging from twelve to forty years of age, who served under the designation Women's Volunteer Workers Corps. The mobilized females were forced to engage in harsh manual labor, and a good many of them were sent to the war zone to work in brothels for Japanese soldiers. According to the accounts of Yoshida Seiji, the Japanese authorities even picked up pregnant women to meet their allocated quotas despite instructions that they draft only single females between the ages of eighteen and twenty-nine.[38]

Most of those Koreans drafted into military service and forced labor abroad were anxious to be repatriated to Korea upon its liberation from Japan after World War II. A mass exodus from Japan to Korea took place from many Japanese ports. Every available seagoing ship was employed, including small fishing vessels. The released conscripts took only whatever belongings they could carry. However, the repatriation operation was ineffective, as the means for getting the Koreans home were limited.

Another factor hindering Korean repatriation was negative reports about conditions in Korea brought back by returning Japanese. They told of riots, strikes, epidemic diseases, floods, and famine. Their stories caused many Koreans in Japan to have second thoughts about returning home, and of 646,932 Koreans who registered for repatriation in March 1946 with the Supreme Command for Allied Powers, 132,897 did not want to leave Japan for Korea.[39] Some repatriates even went back to Japan illegally after their return to Korea because conditions in Korea were so severe.

Nearly 650,000 Koreans who chose not to repatriate believed that they would be able to visit and write their relatives in Korea as often as they wished. During the later stages of the repatriation operation, however, Korea was divided and in 1948 two opposing regimes were established, the pro-American Republic of Korea on August 15 and the pro-Russian Democratic People's Republic of Korea in September. The Korean residents in Japan were not allowed to visit their relatives and friends in Korea unless their ideologies matched the stance of their part of their homeland. In addition, they became polarized ideologically in Japan: Ch'ongnyŏn, joined by 250,000 left-wing Koreans, was organized in 1945 and pledged allegiance to and received financial support from North Korea; Mindan, organized in October 1946, had 350,000 members who registered as nationals of South Korea.

These two uncompromising organizations created another grave problem for Koreans in Japan regarding reunion, visitation, and even communication with relatives in their homeland. During the first ten years of negotiations to normalize relations with Japan, Syngman Rhee, who became the first president of South Korea in 1948, not only failed to support Koreans in Japan but also refused to allow Koreans who belonged to Ch'ongnyŏn to visit or communicate with their relatives in South Korea because of the organization's allegiance to North Korea.

Thus alienated by the South Korean government, the procommunist and left-wing sympathizers of Ch'ongnyŏn played a significant role in mobilizing support for the North Korean regime. Ch'ongnyŏn was able to win Japanese public support for the repatriation of some Korean residents in Japan to North Korea. The Kishi government (1957–1960) of Japan ultimately permitted Koreans who desired repatriation to North Korea to return home. Nearly 100,000 Koreans in Japan repatriated to North Korea.[40]

The quality of life of the repatriated Koreans to North Korea is not well known. After their repatriation they were not allowed to visit relatives in Japan. Consequently, they became separated ultimately from relatives in both Japan and South Korea. Most of these Koreans had come originally from South Korea.[41]

The postwar Korean-Japanese normalization talks, which faltered during the Syngman Rhee administration, were later reopened by the military junta led by Chung-hee Park in 1961. An agreement was reached in 1965, despite demonstrations and public protest rallies against the treaty.[42] At the negotiation table "the ROK government either made no serious effort to or was incapable of exerting its influence to obtain better legal status for its nationals in Japan."[43] The primary concern of the Park regime was to secure financial concessions from Japan.

Nearly 650,000 Korean residents in Japan continue to be subject to discrimination.[44] Most Koreans in Japan have lived there for a prolonged period—some for more than four decades. Approximately three-fourths of their descendants have been born in Japan, and an increasing number of them are third-generation residents. The Japanese exclusion policy against Korean residents has caused various forms of separatism. The Korean community displays almost all the characteristics associated with minorities elsewhere: they are segregated and discriminated against, and they suffer severe economic problems because of their inadequate education and low skill levels. Their way of life, socioeconomic conditions, and legal status in Japanese society are well documented.[45]

KOREANS IN RUSSIA

Even though Korea shares part of its northeastern border with Siberia, formal contact between Russia and Korea did not occur until the middle of the nineteenth century, when Russia joined other countries to place pressure upon the Yi dynasty of Korea to repudiate its policy of isolationism. The power struggle among these competing foreign forces led to the Russo-Japanese War of 1904–1905 on the Korean peninsula. The war that ended with a Japanese victory marked the beginning of Russian involvement in Korean affairs.

Koreans in Russia before the Japanese annexation of Korea in 1910 were illegal immigrants who had left Korea to farm in Russia.[46] By the end of the 1920s the Korean population in Russia, which was mostly concentrated in the Maritime Province, had increased dramatically, from an estimated 50,000 to 310,000. The rise was mainly because of the influx of a large number of Korean refugees seeking political sanctuary from Japanese colonial rule.[47]

The primary concern of this study is the Korean conscripts on Sakhalin Island in the Soviet Union. The Koreans on Sakhalin were originally taken to that island between 1937 and 1945 by the Japanese as a part of their mobilization for war. At one time, the Korean population in Sakhalin reached 150,000. But when the Japanese experienced a shortage of manpower in the battlefields of Southeast Asia near the end of the war, they transferred 100,000 Koreans from the island to various places in Southeast Asian war zones. When World War II ended, Soviet authorities counted 43,000 Koreans on Sakhalin Island.[48] A recent estimate (1982) gives the

A South Korean soldier unaccustomed to American shoes carrying them on a march. From the U.S. Department of the Army, Korea, 1950.

Korean population on Sakhalin as over 60,000, including second- and third-generation descendants.[49]

Theoretically, the Korean conscripts who were taken to Sakhalin by the Japanese should have been repatriated to Korea when World War II ended, but Japan did not make any effort to repatriate them. Koreans forced to go to Sakhalin had been officially classified as Japanese nationals, but when Japan surrendered to the Allied forces and Korea was liberated from Japanese rule, Koreans were consequently no longer considered Japanese nationals and found themselves in a precariously orphaned sta-

Enlisted American soldiers using Korean chi-kae, *or A-frames,*
carry mats, stovepipes, and other gear during the withdrawal
from P'yŏngyang to the thirty-eighth parallel. From the U.S.
Department of the Army, Korea, 1950.

tus. By 1948 their homeland had become divided, and the Soviets, who
had regained control of the island (it had been ceded to Japan during
the Russo-Japanese War), would not allow Koreans there who desired to
be repatriated to South Korea to obtain exit visas or permission to leave
as the East-West Cold War intensified and then war between North and
South Korea erupted. Political pressure was placed on all Koreans on the
island to choose either Russian or North Korean citizenship. They were
told that unless they chose one of the two citizenships, they would be a
denationalized people.[50] The number of Koreans thus denationalized has
been estimated at 6,924.[51] They have been discriminated against by the
Russian authorities because of their unwillingness to choose citizenship in
a communist regime and their wish to be repatriated to noncommunist
countries, either South Korea or Japan.[52]

   According to an official Japanese account in June 1983, Japan has received since 1975 a total of 480 applications to enter Japan from Koreans
on Sakhalin. The Japanese government has granted entry visas to 411, but

because of the refusal of the Soviet authorities to issue exit visas to the applicants, only 3 had been able to come to Japan by June 4, 1983.[53]

While some 5,000 Koreans on Sakhalin wish to be repatriated to South Korea, 1,576 favor being repatriated to Japan.[54] In 1958, led by No-hak Park and P'il-hi Lee, the 3 returnees from Sakhalin organized the Society for the Return of Detainees on Sakhalin (SRDS) and submitted their petition for repatriation to the embassy of South Korea in Tokyo.[55] Their efforts did not produce any positive results other than gaining the support of a few Japanese sympathizers. Even when the Park government of South Korea had been negotiating with Japan for a normalization treaty in the early 1960s, negotiations had not included the repatriation of Koreans on Sakhalin who wished to return to South Korea.[56] The position of the Park government had been basically the same as that of Syngman Rhee.[57]

At the present time, the SRDS in Japan monitors letters from the Korean residents on Sakhalin to their relatives in South Korea. Letters from South Korea to relatives on Sakhalin are usually delivered through the SRDS in Japan because no postal agreement exists between the Soviet Union and South Korea.

DISPERSAL ACROSS THE THIRTY-EIGHTH PARALLEL

Because the origin and development of the Korean War is too broad a subject and because the literature on the war is growing, I will not attempt to relate the course of the war in this book.[58] Instead, I will focus on events before and during the war that affected family dispersal on opposite sides of the thirty-eighth parallel.[59]

After the Soviet Union accepted the proposal to divide the liberated Korean peninsula along the thirty-eighth parallel, Soviet forces entered the area north of that line almost a full month before American forces arrived. Soviet troops reached the parallel by August 24, 1945, and suspended railroad travel and communications between the north and south, prohibiting any exchange of visitors or merchandise. They cut off all telephone and wireless exchanges between North and South Korea beginning September 6, 1945, just two days before the arrival of the United States occupation forces to South Korea.[60] Daily life for Koreans immediately became difficult because of the imbalance of the Korean economy brought about by the Soviet blockade as shipments of products from northern industries and

southern farms virtually ceased. For a short time limited contact between
the north and south was maintained. The supply of electricity from the
north, for example, continued. This limited contact was suspended, however, on May 14, 1948, four days after the general election to form a new
government in the south was held.[61]

Trade between the north and the south was officially prohibited on
March 31, 1949, by the Russian authorities, but small amounts of merchan-
dise kept flowing and widespread smuggling occurred across the border.
Such trade continued through underground channels even after the es-
tablishment of the South Korean government and continued during the
Korean War whenever there was a lull in the fighting.[62]

The exchange of mail between north and south was uncertain during
the period between the wars. Mail delivery was suspended by the Soviet
authorities after September 6, 1945, but then was resumed as a result of
an agreement reached at the US-USSR Joint Commission meeting from
January 16 to February 5, 1946. The first exchange of mail after this took
place at Kaesŏng station on March 15, 1946. The volume of mail sent from
the south to north, amounting to 302,209 pieces, drastically outnumbered
that sent from the north to the south (14,560 pieces).[63] Mail exchange continued even after the formal inaugurations of the different governments in
the south and north in 1948 and lasted until a week prior to the outbreak
of the Korean War.[64] The mails were the only means of contact between
family members separated by the parallel. And even this means of communication was limited by the tendency of letter writers to censor themselves,
to avoid making politically sensitive statements that might endanger family
members on the other side of the fence.

Discussions of the problem of refugees tend to deal with North Koreans
who fled south during the Korean War, but the refugee problem started
well before the outbreak of the war. When North Korea declared democratic reform after the Democratic People's Republic of Korea was formed
in September 1948, many anticommunist nationalists, landowners, intellectuals, clergymen, and young men evading the draft had fled to the
south. From the year of liberation (1945) to the year before the Korean
War (1949), 3.3 million North Koreans, an average of 3,000 per month,
escaped to the south. The exodus continued through the various underground routes until the outbreak of the Korean War in the summer of 1950,
bringing the total finally to 3.5 million.[65] This influx of North Koreans was
a heavy burden on the sagging South Korean economy. The limited job

market of the post-liberation years was incapable of absorbing the massive numbers of refugees, most of whom had to eke out a living. Food for the refugees also presented a serious problem, as did education, since existing school facilities could not meet the needs of so many more children.[66]

When the war began early on Sunday, June 25, 1950, along the thirty-eighth parallel, the South Korean army was caught completely off guard. The South Korean armed forces, vastly inferior to their northern counterparts in manpower and equipment, had to give up Ŭijŏngbu, the gateway to Seoul, on the second day of the war. North Korean tanks reached Seoul on June 28, the third day, and while President Syngman Rhee assured the frightened citizens over the radio that he would make every effort to secure the capital city, the South Korean army blew up the Han River Bridge, cutting off the major route leading south.[67] Over one and a half million Seoulites were thus isolated and trapped, panic-stricken and unable to flee. This thwarted retreat separated many family members.

On June 25, at the request of the United States, the United Nations Security Council had passed a resolution calling for the immediate cessation of hostilities and the withdrawal of the North Korean armed forces to the thirty-eighth parallel. The Soviet delegate was absent.[68] The Security Council also called upon all United Nations members to render every assistance in the execution of its resolution. Concurring were Great Britain, Canada, Australia, New Zealand, the Netherlands, and ten other countries in addition to the United States. These nations promised to send naval and air contingents to Korea. These contingents constituted the United Nations forces.

On June 29 three hundred planes under United Nations command entered the Korean arena, followed by the arrival of United Nations forces in Pusan on July 1. On July 7 the Security Council authorized the unified command in Korea to use the United Nations flag in operations against the north and asked the United States to designate a commander of the unified forces. President Harry S. Truman named Gen. Douglas MacArthur as commander-in-chief of the United Nations forces.[69]

Unfortunately, however, the tide of the war was not to be reversed in a few days. Korea's rainy weather, which had started in July, was a hindrance to a major military operation, and the United Nations forces continued to retreat through July, as North Korean troops advanced farther south and penetrated the Kŭm River line of defense. On July 20, Taejŏn, the temporary capital, fell to the communists, and toward the end of July they occupied the whole southwestern and northeastern sections of the peninsula. Thousands of South Koreans were separated from their family members as a consequence of the march of northern troops southward.

During the period that the communists occupied most of the southern peninsula, they controlled the zone thoroughly and systematically, utilizing well-organized and fully thought-out war plans and deploying large numbers of North Korean security guards. The invaders ferreted out reactionary elements, including members of the South Korean armed forces, police, anticommunist rightists, nationalists, politicians, leaders of various civic and social organizations, landowners, and public officials, who were subject to arrest, imprisonment, abduction, and persecution. Open trials, called people's courts, and kangaroo courts were held to convict the arrested persons at locations that were likely to attract great public attention throughout the occupied southern part of the peninsula. There were innumerable massacres by the communist occupation authorities. At Taejŏn prison, for instance, 1,724 people, including rightists and members of the South Korean military and police and their family members, were ruthlessly massacred, with 300 of them later determined to have been buried alive. At Kwangju prison 300 jailed anticommunists were killed.[70]

The standing committee of the North Korean Supreme People's Congress had issued an ordinance on wartime mobilization on July 1, which forced the residents of the occupied area to collaborate with the People's Army. Volunteer corps, student army corps, youth leagues, and women's leagues were mobilized to recruit volunteers on the street. The number of volunteers recruited and drafted from the entire occupied portion of South Korea was estimated to be approximately 200,000.[71] Many South Korean political leaders, reputable scholars, intellectuals, and prominent writers who were unable to escape Seoul were kidnapped and forcibly taken to the north.

In the midst of this turmoil, on September 15, 1950, General MacArthur's forces made their spectacular amphibious landing at Inch'ŏn, and the tide of war turned abruptly in favor of the United Nations. Seoul was recaptured, and the troops broke out of the Pusan perimeter. As the North Korean army retreated northward, the United Nations forces crossed the thirty-eighth parallel and marched north, securing the area to the Yalu River, which serves as a natural boundary between North Korea and Manchuria.

The war then moved into a new, more complicated stage as the Chinese People's Volunteers (CPV) appeared at the front in October and in late

November. More volunteer forces crossed over from Manchuria and struck in strength, employing so-called human-wave tactics. During the initial CPV attack in late October and the massive Chinese counteroffensive in late November, great numbers of Chinese troops entered North Korea.[72] "The U.N. command estimated that about 486,000 enemy troops, or twenty-one Chinese and twelve North Korean divisions, were committed to the Korean front and that reserves totalling over one million men were stationed near the Yalu, in Manchuria, or on the way to Manchuria."[73]

The CPV and reorganized North Korean troops then halted the advance of the United Nations forces, including South Korean troops, and forced them to withdraw from the area they occupied in North Korea. The United Nations and attached South Korean forces withdrew rapidly to the south, relinquishing P'yŏngyang on December 4. During this retreat, the largest number of North Koreans to flee at one time also moved south, especially from P'yŏngyang and Hŭngnam. Many Koreans refer to this winter retreat as the *ilsa hu-t'oe,* or "January fourth retreat"; however, it actually took place in late November and early December of 1950, not on January 4, 1951, which was when Seoul was taken by the CPV.

The military decision to abandon P'yŏngyang and the flight of P'yŏngyang citizens over the Taedong River produced bedlam. The damaged iron bridge over the river had not yet been fully repaired, and many desperate refugees appeared to be performing acrobatic stunts on the severed and crooked railings of the bridge as they crossed the river. Some fell to their deaths in the stream; others were wounded severely. The refugees, assisted by servicemen, patched up the disconnected bridge parts with wood to provide a scanty crossing. The river was also covered with improvised rafts carrying refugees, and it was estimated that between the evenings of December 4 and 5, 1950, nearly 50,000 refugees crossed the Taedong River.[74] The retreat was equally miserable from the area of the Tumen River in the northeastern part of North Korea. The inhabitants of Hamkyŏng Puk-do and Hamkyŏng Nam-do provinces set out on their southward journey and began to throng such port cities as Sŏngjin, Hamhŭng, Hŭngnam, and Wŏnsan, hoping for sea evacuation.

On December 24, evacuation operations in Hŭngnam were in full swing. To ship as many refugees as possible, for example, a landing ship tank was crammed with 5,000 passengers, ten times the authorized capacity. But the sea operations were unable to evacuate all of the refugees, who numbered between 91,000 and 98,000.[75] Downtown Hŭngnam still overflowed with people who had failed to get aboard ships. Those who could not find room were simply left behind. As witnesses watched in horror, some of the stranded refugees drowned themselves in the sea.[76]

Similar evacuations were taking place in several other ports in early December 1950. The United States Navy evacuated 7,000 refugees from Wŏnsan and 12,000 from Sŏngjin in Hamkyŏng Puk-do province.[77] Thirty thousand were evacuated by sea from Chin'nampo on the west coast.[78] From the west coast alone the total number of evacuees reached 62,082.[79] During the period from December 1950 to the end of January 1951, the total number of North Korean refugees amounted to nearly 1 million.[80]

For the refugees a more serious problem than bitter cold, starvation, and disease was their position behind the retreating soldiers. The soldiers were using military vehicles while most of the refugees had to trudge along on foot during their long journey. Far outdistanced by the fast-retreating military forces, the refugees were often subject to raids and harrassment by communist guerrillas. Worse than anything else was family dispersal, as many refugees had to leave one or more members of their families in the north. Some had no time to get in touch with family members in the thick of the war; others were lost or separated from their families on the way south.

When Chinese troops crossed the thirty-eighth parallel and entered Seoul on January 4, 1951, the South Korean government and the United Nations troops pulled out of Seoul and abandoned the port of Inch'ŏn. Once again they had to face the evacuation of refugees. The war during the winter months of 1951 consisted of attacks and counterattacks to the south of Seoul, and in early March the United Nations troops began to make substantial gains and move steadily forward. Then, on the nights of March 14 and 15, United Nations troops moved once more into Seoul, which by now had changed hands four times. The United Nations forces fought their way to the thirty-eighth parallel, and on April 4 they broke through that line, opening the door for a northward march. On April 11 President Truman relieved General MacArthur of his command and replaced him with General Ridgway.[81] Under Ridgway's command the United Nations troops and South Korean forces successfully brought the Chinese and North Korean forces to a standstill, and from May 20 to June 24, 1951, the United Nations and South Korean forces advanced against generally light resistance. Except in the west where they had veered southward to take tactical advantage of the Imjin River, the United Nations and South Korean army lines had pushed the invading forces north of the thirty-eighth parallel. South Korea was thus virtually cleared of the communist forces.

TABLE I
Dispersed Koreans

Cause of Dispersal	Current Location	Estimated Number
Japanese mobilization	Sakhalin, Russia	40,000
Emergence of the 38th parallel (after liberation from Japan and before the Korean War)	South Korea	3,500,000
Retreat from occupied North Korea	South Korea	1,000,000
Kidnapped by North Korea	North Korea	84,000
Release of anticommunist prisoners of war	South Korea	27,663
Repatriation to North Korea by Japan	North Korea	100,000
Hijackings and seizures of planes and vessels	North Korea	400
Reported missing during the Korean War	Unknown	300,000
Total		5,052,063

SOURCES: *Hankook Ilbo,* July 6, 1983; *Dong-A Ilbo, Ah! Sara issöttguna* (Oh! You were alive after all) (Seoul: Dong-A Ilbo, 1983), 281–284.

As the tide of the war turned in favor of the United Nations, the Soviet Union proposed ceasefire discussions between the participants in the Korean War. The Truman administration was eager to end the war, now that it was possible to establish a division of Korea near the thirty-eighth parallel.[82] When the rulers of China indicated their interest in a truce, Truman authorized General Ridgway to begin negotiating with enemy generals. The talks opened on July 10, 1951, at Kaesŏng. On July 27, 1953, at P'anmunjŏm, despite the disapproval of a large number of South Koreans led by President Syngman Rhee, an agreement was finally reached on terms for an armistice. Each side would pull its forces behind the demilitarized zone established between the battle lines in effect at the time of the armistice. Prisoners of war were exchanged, and the Neutral Nations Supervision Commission was set up to ensure that both sides adhered to the agreement.

This agreement stopped the fighting; however, the war had created millions of dispersed families. South Koreans, including political leaders, intellectuals, and reporters, rhetorically refer to *il-ch'ŏn-man isan kajok,* or "ten million dispersed families." This figure is double the estimated 5 million dispersed family members (see table 1), emphasizing that one family separated became two separate (north and south) families.

The estimated figure of 5 million in table 1 appears reasonable but it should be carefully considered. For example, of the 3.5 million North Koreans who fled south before the Korean War, a good many were not dispersed in the true sense because often entire families were able to flee together, or at least their nuclear units were able to. They may have been relocated or displaced, but they were not dispersed families. If this argument is valid, the estimated number is probably overstated, but a completely accurate figure would still reveal the devastating results of Korea's modern history.

CHAPTER 3

Korean Family and Kinship

I do not intend to review the Korean family and kinship system in detail,[1] but a brief description of the principles of Korean kinship may help those who are unfamiliar with them understand how separation affected the Korean family. Every human being is related to other human beings and behaves on the basis of many principles, but for Koreans the principle of kinship is foremost.[2]

The Chinese influence of Confucianism on Korean kinship was strongest among the nobility (*yangban*),[3] especially during the Yi dynasty (1392–1910). Thus, ideal patterns of Korean kinship were similar to those of the Chinese. Yet, the customs regulating kinship and family relations of non-noble commoners, who were not deeply imbued with the Confucian virtues, differed from those of nobles. In this discussion, however, ideal patterns of Korean kinship serve as the frame of reference.

In the past, marriages in Korea were thoroughly arranged, particularly among the noble class, who used marriage to maintain their status quo.[4] During the Yi dynasty, the system of arranged marriages contributed to class endogamy, in which most Koreans married within their own class. Up until the most recent times, two modified forms of arrangement have been used. In one the person selects several candidates and then asks his or her parents to choose from among them. In the other parents and kin recommend several candidates almost equal in their qualifications for final selection by the person who is going to be married. Arranged marriages are still popular in rural Korean villages, although an increasing number of young, educated, and urban Koreans freely choose their own partners. Even in cities, however, the so-called *madam-ttu,* who arranges marriages between children of a newly rich and privileged class, has emerged, replacing the traditional matchmaker or go-between. Such semiprofessional matchmakers charge such high commissions for their services that they have become a social problem.[5]

The ideal form of marriage in Korea was and is monogamy, but polygyny (the marriage of one man to two or more women at the same time) and concubinage have been institutionalized since the beginning of the Samhan era around the first century B.C., particularly for those who needed male heirs. Despite denial of the existence of a plural spouse system in the South Korean civil code,[6] nearly 2 percent of the contemporary Korean population still practices polygyny.[7]

Upon marriage, following the patrilocal rule of residence, a newlywed couple traditionally lives with or near the parents or the grandparents of the groom. Currently, many young Korean couples establish their own independent residences. Nevertheless, many firstborn sons and their brides still tend to live with the groom's parents. This trend has been further enhanced by the development of the stem family, which is a form of family in transition from the extended family to the nuclear family. Particularly in rural Korea, one son, usually the firstborn son, remains home with his parents (and brings in his bride when he marries), while the other sons move elsewhere to establish their own nuclear families.

In Korea, because marriage transfers the bride to the groom's family, her adjustment to married life may be difficult. She is expected to master the family's routines and recipes. No one in the husband's family will extend sympathy to a young bride.[8] Her life may become hard to endure because often the mother-in-law exercises absolute authority over her daughter-in-law, especially during the initial stage of adjustment after the marriage, called *sijib sari*. Even if the demands of her mother-in-law are unreasonable, difficult, and even harsh, the daughter-in-law has to obey. Otherwise, her behavior is interpreted as unfilial to her parents-in-law; at one time this was grounds for divorce. The husband traditionally remains neutral or takes the side of his mother, not the side of his wife. This is more prevalent in *yangban* families, because they are more inclined to conform to socioethical ideals.

The traditional authority pattern of the Korean family is patriarchal, which allocates authority to the males. The evolution of the South Korean civil code toward the achievement of equal rights and privileges for men and women has occurred at least as a matter of law if not of practice. Such legislation is a major accomplishment in a society in which power and authority have so long been vested in the males, with the oldest male usually wielding the greatest power.

The authority inherent in the relationship of parents to their children, particularly of father to son, is of the utmost importance. The relationship between father and son is governed by the virtue of filial piety (*hyo'sŏng* in Korean and *hsiao* in Chinese). "The Twenty-Four Examples of Filial Piety" are well-known tales governing the Chinese practice of filial piety that have instructed and entertained the Chinese for many centuries.[9] Korean moral axioms regarding filial piety are not any less numerous than their Chinese counterparts and may even outnumber them, especially after the seventh and eighth centuries. The Chinese classic on filial piety, *Hsia Ching* (*Hyo Kyŏng* in Korean), was the first textbook adopted by Koreans.[10] The accounts of filial piety in Korean society can be easily found in folk tales about the feeding and care of aged parents.[11] "Included were stories of sons who fed their own flesh and blood to their ailing parents."[12] Even now, many women in rural Korean villages consider stories of filial piety more instructive for their children than any other story or tale.[13] Disobeying one's parents, especially the father, is a violation of filial piety and a challenge to their authority.

The patriarchal rules are closely related to the position of women in the Korean family system in particular and in Korean society in general, and they set the tone of sexual discrimination in that society. Because of male preference, a good many Korean parents discriminate against their daughters. Roger L. Janelli and Dawnhee Yim Janelli heard about female infanticide during their fieldwork in a rural Korean village, although it occurs rarely nowadays: "One lineage woman, in the presence of her seven- or eight-year-old maternal granddaughter, told us how she had placed the girl on a cold floor immediately after birth, hoping she would die." The woman unhesitatingly said, "But look how well she grew up."[14] Unwanted female babies were sometimes abandoned at the gate of a stranger's house.[15] Even in ancestral worship, "women were excluded from officiating at the rites, and ritual responsibility could not be assumed by a wife or a daughter's son in the absence of an agnatically related male heir."[16] Clark W. Sorensen has observed that "At meals . . . women serve the men first, in sequence by status and seniority within the family."[17]

The marital bond in Korean kinship is strong. Even if spouses have been physically separated, because of the war, for example, the marital bond between them is often sustained. Some dispersed spouses have maintained their marital status for over three decades. The strong marital bond in Korean kinship is reflected in the practice of divorce among Koreans. For a *yangban* woman, seeking divorce is traditionally considered dishonorable toward her natal family. This is not to say that divorce does not exist in Korea, but it is uncommon. It is male-centered, influenced during the Yi dynasty by Confucian teachings and the Ta Ming Lu, the criminal code developed during the Ming dynasty (1368–1644).[18]

Based on the Ta Ming Lu, Koreans derived the three rules of obedience, which state that a woman must follow her parents in youth, follow her husband in marriage, and follow her sons in old age, and the seven evil causes of divorce, which allow a man to divorce his wife when she is disobedient to his parents, fails to bear a child or children, commits adultery, succumbs to jealousy, contracts a repulsive disease, offends with her loquacity, or steals from the family, usually to help her natal mother. To avoid excessive male-centered divorce, Koreans developed the three provisions against divorcing a wife: she has no one to depend on if expelled from the husband's household; she has borne with her husband the three-year mourning period for his deceased parents; or the man has gone from poverty to wealth since marrying her.[19]

After the fall of the Yi dynasty and under Japanese colonial rule, male-centered norms regulating divorce persisted because of similar values held by the Japanese. After liberation from Japan and influenced by Western concepts of egalitarianism, the South Korean civil code denoted specific conditions for divorce that were equally applicable to men and women. Adultery, however, was still limited to only the wife's transgressions. The infidelity of a husband was not recognized as adultery until a fairly recent revision of the civil code.[20]

In an extensive study of divorce cases presented in the Seoul District Court during the ten years after the liberation of Korea from Japan in 1945, T'ae-yŏng Lee found a total of 144 divorces. Except for a few cases, the defendants were women. This study focused on the heart of urban South Korea but still revealed a male monopoly in divorce suits. If the study had been done in rural districts, male domination in divorce would have been even greater.[21]

In February 1962 Jai-seuk Choi made a survey of two apartment complexes in Seoul and three rural villages in different South Korean provinces to diagnose the attitudes of Korean people toward divorce. In Seoul, concerning wife abuse, 35.2 percent of the women responding indicated that they would remain patient and take abuses, and 21.4 percent said they would seek a separation to avoid abuse. In the rural villages 67.9 percent indicated that there would be no choice but to endure abuse while hoping for better relations in the future, and only 5.4 percent would seek separation.[22]

The rule of descent in Korea is patrilineal, which affiliates an individual with a group of kinsmen, all of whom are related to him or her through male lines. Its origin in Korea may even be prehistoric, but the patrilineal rule of descent was strengthened under Chinese influence at the beginning of the Three Kingdoms period, around the first half of the first century B.C. It strengthened further during the early seventeenth century.[23] Since this rule requires tracing one's kin relationships through males, it has fostered the concept of male preference. The close relationship between the increase of the Korean population and the Korean custom of male preference is well documented.[24] Many Koreans of childbearing age will continue to give birth to children until they have at least one son.

To uphold the patrilineal descent rule, when families were heirless, either having daughters only or no children at all, they sometimes tried polygynous arrangements, although such instances are limited nowadays. Most often they would adopt a male for an heir, but the range of choices for the adoption was very limited. Over the last few centuries, Koreans have preferred to adopt male heirs from agnates (persons related by patrilineal descent).[25] Despite a revision of the South Korean civil code in 1977 that permitted adoption of someone with a different surname and the entry of the husband's name into his wife's family register, Koreans have still adhered to a strict agnatic principle. This practice is beginning to change.[26]

Most of all, the Korean patrilineal rule of descent gave rise to a number of elaborate kin groups, lineages, and clans (made up of related lineages).[27] There are 1,100 clans in Korea, each of which includes scores of lineages.[28] However, how many Koreans are actually affiliated with active lineages or clans is difficult to ascertain.[29] Most *yangban* Koreans are members of some lineages.

The most important mechanism for promoting a sense of belonging to a kin group is the extensive use of kinship terms to encompass the entire membership of the kin group, the basic medium being the genealogical record.[30] One addresses other members by using kinship terms, regardless of how remote the relationship may be. The Korean expression *ilgabaekdae chi ch'in* means that members of the same lineage or even the same clan are all kin even after many generations removed from the common ancestor.

Such an attitude toward the kin group is further fostered by participation in worship of the common ancestor and in communal ownership of property. Regarding the communal property of a lineage, each member feels that he is an owner of that lineage property, even if he is too poor to own property as an individual. In the rural Korean village where I did fieldwork some years ago, a lineage owned three different communal properties: ritual land for the lineage; land for the support of formal education for capable young members; and land for the common welfare of all the members.[31] If a young member is brilliant and capable of pursuing further education but cannot afford the expense, the lineage supports such an individual in the form of a scholarship provided by profits from the school land.

The idea of supporting the education of the young members of the lineage is based on the belief that if they obtain high positions in government or gain prominence as scholars, prestige and fame are automatically bestowed on the entire membership of the lineage. The Chinsŏng Lee lineage (in this case clan is more appropriate than lineage) has enjoyed its *yangban* privileges because an ancestor, Yi Hwang (or T'oegye, 1501–1570), was noted for his scholarship and became a prominent figure in the history of philosophy in Korea. Likewise, the members of the P'ungsan Yu lineage have *yangban* status because their ancestor Yu Sŏng-nyong (or Sŏae, 1542–1607) was also a noted scholar.[32] During the Yi dynasty, this system was fully demonstrated by certain lineages, and although social patterns of contemporary Korea differ significantly from those during the Yi dynasty, the idea that the success and honor of one member of a lineage means success and honor for the entire lineage lingers for many Koreans who belong to the active and prosperous lineages.

For many North Korean refugees such kinship ties were broken by the wars and the partition of the nation. Some have tried to fulfill that relationship by assembling and mobilizing their kin members wherever they have been relocated. Reflecting the importance of kinship to Koreans, those without a kin group affiliation have created pseudo, quasi, or fictional kinships, basing their ties on having attended the same school or coming from the same prefecture. The offices of North Korean provisional provinces in the south play a similar role, joining people in groups. Fictional kinship is much more prevalent among the North Korean refugees in the south.

My own work on Korean immigrants in a southern city of the United States revealed that "they create new fictional kin among their close friends and address one another using these kin terms. Some of these people move into the same apartment complex, i.e., public housing complexes, and develop gregarious living patterns. . . . This serves as an important mechanism in their adjustment to the new environment."[33] North Korean refugees also used such adaptive strategies as they adjusted to life in South Korea.

Parenthetically, as another indication of the importance of one's kin group affiliation, the Red Cross application form for the reunion telethon contained a blank column for the applicant's kin group affiliation.

The rule of inheritance in Korea has changed over a long period of time. Following the rule of primogeniture, the eldest or firstborn son normally assumes the headship of the family and inherits his parents' property. Prior to the 1600s, however, the rule allowed sons and daughters to inherit equally, without any discrimination by sex, as was the case in China. After the 1600s Korean law began favoring sons, discriminating against daughters. Since the 1800s the eldest son has been favored, to form a classic primogeniture system, which is the ideal of Korean inheritance. But, ultimogeniture, a system in which the youngest son inherits the family's estate is not uncommon among people who have only a marginal livelihood and in some remote mountain villages.[34]

During Japanese domination, laws governing Korean kinship and the family were mainly based on the existing Korean norms.[35] Even after liberation, the South Korean civil code regulating the rules of inheritance reflected traditional norms by discriminating against females (daughters) and by favoring males, particularly the eldest son. The version of the civil code revised in 1977, despite an effort to upgrade the position of women in inheritance, gives 5 percent more to the eldest son than to other sons and to unmarried daughters. If a daughter has married and moved out of her natal home, she receives only a quarter of the allotment given to her brothers.[36] Strong social norms still determine who receives inherited property and how it is allocated: offspring of a formal wife inherit over those born to a secondary wife; eldest sons inherit over younger sons; and sons inherit over daughters.

All the rules and regulations of Korean kinship—patrilineal descent, patrilocal residence, patriarchal authority, primogeniture, arranged marriage, discouragement of divorce, the presence of polygyny and concubinage, and male preference—have fostered the continuity of Korean kinship.[37] Traditionally in Korea such continuity has taken precedence over "love" or "sex appeal" or other characteristics. Francis L. K. Hsu's term "asexuality," meaning "the condition of having no connection with sex," can be applied to Korean kinship.[38] In the past a woman's sex appeal, charm, and beauty were not important in the selection of a bride. Instead, Koreans used morphological features considered conducive to childbearing, especially to the bearing of male children. Those features, according to Kyu-t'ae Lee, included "long and narrow eyebrows," "broad hips with a large stomach," and "light and bright skin color,"[39] and they took precedence in choosing a future bride. The woman's reproductive role in continuing the family line of her husband was of the utmost importance.

Sexual subjects cannot be touched upon even casually in any decent conversation. Discussions of sex cannot find a place in any literature other than pornography. Other taboos go even further. Even married couples do not display any sign of intimacy between them. A kiss in a public or semi-public place is hardly seen even nowadays in Korea. A kiss between husband and wife before parents and relatives, particularly with elderly members present, is unthinkable. Ideally, a couple remains aloof to each other. Their duties and obligations toward their parents and elders are more important than their own interests. Amazingly, no reunited husbands and wives during the reunion telethon kissed each other, and most of them did not even hug each other when they were reunited. One can entertain the hypothesis that, if the Korean kinship system were not asexual, not many dispersed Korean husbands and wives would have avoided remarriage.

The Korean War brought about cultural change in Korea along with unprecedented economic growth in the south. One specific result of the war alone—family dispersal—has significantly altered one aspect of Korean culture. The massive emigration, mainly from north to south, during the war has helped eliminate the persistent regional feelings and hostilities accumulated throughout Korean history and expand the spheres of marriage, especially between northerners and southerners. Nowadays, marriage between people from different areas of the north and south are common. Not mentioning other factors that have effected change, the war that caused 5 million people to be separated from their families, 300,000 widows and 100,000 orphans, without any doubt has influenced the attitudes of Koreans toward the traditional norms regulating chastity and remarriage.

The figures are unknown, yet I speculate that thousands of widows, widowers, and sundered couples have remarried, even though many dispersed couples still remain single. In turn, people are more tolerant of alternative ethics that go against traditional mores. If a family was to be dispersed now, the responses and reactions of the separated members might be different because of the relaxation of traditional norms. Nevertheless, it is presumptuous and even inaccurate to imply that the fundamental Korean mores regulating Korean family and kinship have been replaced by Western values.

As an analogy, while I was looking around at the scenery of Seoul, I was amazed by the striking parallels between the structural contrasts of different types of buildings and the ethical contrasts. If one focuses on a certain section of downtown Seoul, it looks like any Western city, with high-rise office buildings and hotels. But if one walks along the northern district of Chongro-ku and the foothills of Pukak Mountain, one can find nothing but the thatched roofs of traditional homes. If one concludes that Seoul is no longer a Korean capital by having seen high-rise buildings only, one has failed to see the other side of Seoul.

If, after observing the daily activities of middle-class Seoulites, who wear Western-style clothes, drive their own cars, and live in Western-style apartment complexes, one concludes that they are just like Westerners, one has neglected to note what they do after they come home from work. When they come home, they take off their Western clothes, they sit on the floor even though they have complete sets of Western furniture in their apartments, and they commend their family members in accordance with the traditional Korean family and kinship rules. But they are contemporary Koreans.

Many Korean lineages have launched campaigns to update their genealogies as symbolic reflections of kinship revitalization. Gatherings of lineages occur more often than ever before, despite the increasing participation of Koreans in various formal organizations. Walking along the streets of Seoul, one can easily find more signs indicating the offices of lineages than signs of Rotary, Kiwanis, and Lions clubs. Recently, I received a copy of my lineage genealogy even though I have lived "in this world" for more than twenty years.

The story of Su-kwan Sim, a fourteenth-generation descendant of a Korean in Japan, relates the deeply rooted kinship identity of Koreans.[40] Su-kwan's fourteenth-generation ascending great-grandfather, Tang-kil Sim, was a Korean artisan who manufactured porcelain. Tang-kil was captured by the Japanese in 1597 during the second invasion of Korea by Toyotomi Hideyoshi and was forcibly taken to Japan. Tang-kil settled in Nawashiro, a village in Kagoshima and worked in the manufacture of porcelain. Nearly four centuries later his descendant, Su-kwan, began searching for his kinship identity. In 1964 Su-kwan was able to trace Tang-kil back to Namwŏn in Chŏlla Nam-do province in South Korea, where his ancestor had been captured by the Japanese. He further traced the genealogy of the Ch'ŏngsong Sim clan. Subsequently, Su-kwan found the original village of his ancestors, went there, and observed ancestral rites at the graves of his common ancestors of the Ch'ŏngsong Sim clan. He often visits his ancestral land and has shared his kin relationships with his clan members.

Patrilineal rule supported by primogeniture, a patriarchal authority pattern, and emphasis on asexuality remain strong despite the challenge by modernization, industrialization, and Westernization. Observing this reminded me of a statement, seemingly applicable to Korea, by W. J. Cash concerning change in the American South: "The South, one might say, is a tree with many age rings, with its limbs and trunk bent and twisted by all the winds of the years, but with its tap root in the Old South."[41] The basic attributes of Korean kinship, although "bent and twisted . . . by the years," still have their "tap roots" in ancient Korean tradition.

CHAPTER 4

An Elderly Mother
Longs for Her Son

P'il-yŏ Lee was separated from her son, who was mobilized by the Japanese authorities, during World War II. Since their continued separation is closely related to the partition of Korea after World War II and to the Korean War, her life history has been included in this book. It exemplifies the dispersal of Korean families that occurred even before the Korean War.

P'il-yŏ is a distant relative of mine. To conceal her identity, I am using a pseudonym for her and am also camouflaging our exact relationship. I have known her most of my life, and my sisters and my brother's wife are very good friends of P'il-yŏ's daughter, Sun-ok. Because of these relationships, during my fieldwork they invited me for meals.

Most of the factual information about P'il-yŏ has been collected through other relatives. When I visited P'il-yŏ's home, either one of my sisters or my sister-in-law came along, because I had difficulty finding my way around Seoul. In turn, their presence became another mechanism to check the validity of the information I was gathering.

My interviews with P'il-yŏ took place informally in her home either during or after meals. To avoid disrupting the natural flow of our conversations, I made my own brief notes and did not use a tape recorder.

P'il-yŏ Lee is eighty-two years old (as of 1983). Her life has never been easy, and she has weathered many adversities. She was born into a wealthy *yangban* family but happened to be the daughter of one of four co-wives in a son-hungry polygynous family, so her birth was not really considered a blessing. Soon after her marriage she was discarded by her libidinous husband, who had acquired a concubine. Nearly forty years ago she was separated from her only son, Ch'ang-ho Park, by the Japanese mobilization. P'il-yŏ is still waiting for his return, maintaining her magnanimous manners and elegant appearance, which reflect her noble origin.

Despite having endured hardships throughout her life, she looks younger than her age and appears to be in remarkably good health. Except for her slightly curved back and wrinkled forehead, she has kept herself very well. She has most of her teeth and possesses excellent vision. She does not wear eyeglasses and even dyes her hair regularly. In regard to her good health, P'il-yŏ politely stated her secret in simple terms: "I just take care of myself. I want to live long, so that I can meet my son. I know that people say 'Why does that old woman dye her hair?' I don't do that to make myself look young, better, or anything like that. But I am doing it because I do not want to show my decrepit old face to my son when he returns." She firmly believes that her son will be back tomorrow or within the next few days, even though she has not heard from him for over forty years. Waiting for her son's return has almost become her religion. Her good health seems to be motivated by her noble maternal spirit; her determination to wait for her son may be what keeps her going.

P'il-yŏ was born in 1901 in Ta-dong, the northeastern section of Kyŏng-sang Puk-do province, in the southeastern corner of the Korean peninsula, an area that boasts many *yangban* villages. Ta-dong is composed of members of a single predominant lineage. Most of them are related to each other and share a common surname. Residents in Ta-dong whose surnames are other than Lee are considered commoners (*sangmin*) or members of a despised class, the *ch'ŏnmin*.[1]

In Ta-dong, P'il-yŏ's father, Chae-do Lee, had gained a reputable bureaucratic post in the government of the Yi dynasty by passing the civil service examination, called *kwagŏ*, the major route to becoming a literati-bureaucrat in the Yi dynasty. Examinees of the *kwagŏ* had to demonstrate their scholarship, consisting chiefly of mastery of the Confucian classics. In the Yi dynasty of Korea, as in dynastic China, scholarship led to bureaucratic power, which in turn brought wealth and prestige.

P'il-yŏ told me about the scholarship displayed by her father in passing such a difficult examination. Other relatives told me that P'il-yŏ's father was not scholarly enough to pass the *kwagŏ*, and that he had bought his title (peerage) at the end of the Yi dynasty when the court was becoming corrupt. In fact, a good many wealthy Koreans bought such titles in the early 1900s. Whether her father had bought his title or had attained it through merit was not an important issue for this project, so I did not ask P'il-yŏ about it to avoid possible embarrassment.

At any rate, Chae-do had been remarkably successful in every way except in producing an heir to continue his family. He married four times, but none of his wives was able to conceive a son and heir for him. He took P'il-yŏ's mother, Mundong-daek, as his fourth wife, but she gave birth only to P'il-yŏ.

Chae-do's strong desire for a son is even evident in his name for his young daughter. Her real name denotes something like "no more daughters," reflecting Chae-do's hope that he would be spared the birth of another girl. Furthermore, it is a clear manifestation of the discrimination against women in Korean society in its deviation from traditional Korean naming patterns.

Naming patterns before Korea's contact with Chinese culture are unknown because of the absence of a written language in Korea. Chinese naming patterns are assumed to have been introduced in the early Silla dynasty (57 B.C.–A.D. 668) by Koreans returning from studying in China and have been accepted as traditional Korean naming patterns.[2] The nicknames most commonly received by girls, such as small baby, flat face, and jade princess, are thought to be remnants of the earlier Korean naming system, based on linguistic evidence of the spoken language, and Cornelius Osgood has pointed out that before the Japanese annexation of Korea, Korean girls did not receive proper names but only nicknames.[3] Also, before the impact of Japanese naming patterns, traditional Korean names were characteristically not sex-specific; thus, any name could be conferred upon males or females, as is common among the Eskimo.[4]

P'il-yŏ has not only been discriminated against because of her gender, she also has suffered from being the daughter of a secondary wife. In polygynous arrangements in Korea certain discriminatory practices against the secondary wives and their offspring have occurred. The first wife is treated as the formal wife, and the other co-wives are dealt with as secondary wives, even if they were officially married in wedding ceremonies. The co-wives are expected to respect the first wife, addressing her with the same kinship term that is used to address one's older sister. If a secondary wife gives birth to a male heir, her status is upgraded drastically, and her new status is conferred on her son. A daughter born to a secondary wife, however, will suffer due to the mother's continued secondary status.

Such a secondary status is usually manifested in the marriage arrangements made for female offspring. The reputation, wealth, and prestige of P'il-yŏ's father were sufficient to permit the choice of the best matrimonial candidate for her, but her secondary status was a strong liability. She had to settle for a less desirable candidate than someone who had been born to a formal wife.

A groom named Ch'il-sŏng Park was selected for P'il-yŏ, and as usual in a strict arranged marriage, P'il-yŏ was unable to meet her future husband. Because she was not allowed to see him even at a distance before her marriage, she had no personal knowledge of Ch'il-sŏng. Some people talked negatively about him. He was two years younger than P'il-yŏ and poor, though he was of *yangban* origin. He was incapable of earning a living, having had no formal education and possessing no specific skills. P'il-yŏ's parents believed, however, that even though Ch'il-sŏng might not be a capable person, he would be able to make a proper living if they gave him a sufficient amount of farmland.

P'il-yŏ asked me, "What would you have done in my position?" She answered for me by saying, "I guess most youngsters nowadays would not marry." She indicated that she could not do anything other than grumble about it, but customs required that bridal candidates not even talk about their impending marriage, good or bad. Despite her resentment and reservations, P'il-yŏ's wedding was set. She had to marry Ch'il-sŏng.

P'il-yŏ's marriage was hardly a happy one. As soon as they married, her parents allocated several acres of farmland for P'il-yŏ and her husband, but it was not enough for them. Ch'il-sŏng, prodded by his parents, would ask P'il-yŏ to get more money from her parents. P'il-yŏ then had to visit her parents' home to ask for assistance. If she returned with less money than he had hoped for, Ch'il-sŏng did not hesitate to beat her. These uneasy trips to her natal home continued until she had her first child, a son they called Ch'ang-ho.

By the time P'il-yŏ had a second child, a girl named Sun-ok, the land that P'il-yŏ had brought with her when she married had been transferred to a local usurer because Ch'il-sŏng was unable to repay loans from the usurer that had resulted from his gambling and drinking. Ch'il-sŏng was often away from home, sometimes for months. Finally, Ch'il-sŏng brought his barmaid mistress home, and they lived together with P'il-yŏ. Her husband spent most of his time with his mistress, ignoring P'il-yŏ's existence.

As the days and months went by, quarrels between Ch'il-sŏng and P'il-yŏ, and between P'il-yŏ and the co-wife, became frequent and more violent. Ch'il-sŏng's beating of P'il-yŏ was almost a daily routine, and she suffered bruises all over her body. His abuse was mainly due to her refusal to bring more money from her natal home. No matter how forcefully Ch'il-sŏng demanded, P'il-yŏ would not go to get any more. The situation was becoming too severe to endure.

Ch'il-sŏng's surly mood and his ruthless treatment of P'il-yŏ continued until her parents passed away. Their property was inherited by their adopted son (a former cousin of P'il-yŏ had become her brother by adoption). It was difficult for P'il-yŏ to ask her adopted brother for assistance.

Even under such circumstances, divorce was unthinkable for P'il-yŏ. Traditional Korean custom does not allow a woman to ask for a divorce. "While men could obtain a divorce if they had their parents' consent and had due reason, women were not entitled to initiate divorce *under any circumstance*" (emphasis added).[5] Because Koreans have traditionally viewed marriage as a union between entire families, not just a union between two individuals, divorce is considered the separation of two families.

Thus, after ten years of an unhappy marriage, instead of seeking a divorce, P'il-yŏ left her husband, and taking her children with her, went to a large city to seek employment. To return to her natal home permanently after marriage, whatever the reason, is not respectable for a *yangban* woman. P'il-yŏ wandered all over the city looking for a job but was unable to find one. She was ill prepared for work; she had no specific job skills nor any formal education. Even worse, she was unable to speak Japanese, which at that time was essential for acquiring a job. Having been informed of the hardships of his sister and her children, her brother brought them back to Ta-dong to support them. Although this was a sort of homecoming for P'il-yŏ, it was under the worst of circumstances. Ta-dong brought back memories of the environment in which her parents had chosen to shelter her from matters of the outside world.

P'il-yŏ missed her deceased parents, but her adopted brother and his wife were kind and helpful. They did everything they could to support P'il-yŏ and her children, sending the children to school and paying all the school expenses. P'il-yŏ's dependency upon her brother made her uncomfortable, but it was much more tolerable than living with her husband and his mistress. Her children liked their uncle and aunt. Their uncle acted as if he were their father. Growing up under the same roof gave P'il-yŏ's children and their cousins a common bond, like that of siblings.

When P'il-yŏ's son, Ch'ang-ho, became twenty years old, his uncle arranged a marriage with an eighteen-year-old bride in order to make sure that the family line would continue no matter what happened to the boy's father. Ch'ang-ho's bride came from a decent family background, although the family was not well off. Ch'ang-ho's uncle leased several acres of farmland for Ch'ang-ho to support his family. Assisted by his uncle, Ch'ang-ho and his new bride, together with P'il-yŏ and Sun-ok, managed to acquire their own housing. Although Ch'ang-ho's father was absent from this newly formed, independent household, the continuity of his family was still assured. However, their peaceful interlude did not last long. One day Ch'ang-ho's father suddenly appeared and asked that he be allowed to live with them.

Ch'il-sŏng was unable to maintain his mistress any longer and was alone. He could find no one else to turn to but his wife and children. He was still Ch'ang-ho's father, no matter what he had done to P'il-yŏ and their children. If Ch'ang-ho rejected his father, he would be violating the most fundamental Confucian ethic, that of filial piety, the prime virtue in the Korean mind.[6] At the same time, Ch'ang-ho knew that his father's return was unacceptable to his mother. She was furious about the arrangement and would not stand for it. Although Ch'il-sŏng was never allowed to live permanently in Ch'ang-ho's home, he would stay on and off for a few days at a time, disrupting the entire household.

Ch'ang-ho was in deep anguish. His wife did not know what to do either, for she was caught in the middle of this delicate situation. The family was again in domestic chaos. As the family disturbances intensified, Ch'ang-ho spent more and more time in town drinking with his friends to escape the unpleasant family dilemma. He often came home in a drunken state.

In late September 1943 Ch'ang-ho left home after a family altercation, and after more than a week he still had not returned home. Although he had spent nights away from home before, this was the first time he had been away this long without telling anyone what he was doing. Ch'ang-ho's wife was, of course, worried about her husband, but she could not express her feelings in the presence of her parents-in-law. It would not have been proper for her to display her frustrations or concerns about the safety of her husband any more than it would have been to display affectionate behavior with her husband in front of her parents-in-law or any elderly persons. In this regard, P'il-yŏ's behavior seemed to be governed by two contrasting ethical principles. Although she had a traditional and aristocratic background and was from a conservative region in Korea ideologically, she was almost revolutionary when she refused to live with her husband when he returned to her. However, she was very traditional in dealing with her daughter-in-law, although even in those years, relationships between mothers-in-law and their daughters-in-law were improving. (In the West the word *mother-in-law* often has a negative connotation, usually referring to the delicate relationship between son-in-law and mother-in-law. In Korea it refers exclusively to the uneasy relationship between a man's wife and his mother. In contrast to the West, in Korea the relationship between the son-in-law and the mother-in-law is known to be very easy, relaxed, and friendly.)

P'il-yŏ went to town to search for her son, where she learned that he had volunteered for the Work Corps and would be sent to Sakhalin Island. According to the accounts of one of Ch'ang-ho's friends, who had witnessed the scene, Ch'ang-ho had not joined the Work Corps voluntarily, but had been forced. Frustrated by his domestic situation and in a drunken state, Ch'ang-ho had made the mistake of saying, "I wish I could join the Work Corps. It would be better than having family quarrels all the time." In those days Japanese propaganda promising high wages was used extensively to recruit Korean workers. The promised wages, nearly five times higher than those of industrial workers in the large cities of Korea, seemed a large sum to Korean peasants. In response to such propaganda, whenever they were frustrated some Koreans would exclaim, "I'm going to join the Work Corps!" Even teenagers used the statement to resist their parents. Ch'ang-ho was overheard by a Korean policeman working for the Japanese mobilization authorities and was taken to the police station immediately, to the office of the prefect. He was still quite drunk and did not know what was going on.

This was a time when Japan desperately needed manpower to support the war. In mobilizing Koreans, the Japanese government issued call-up papers. (The paper calling up people to serve in the labor forces was white; the paper for military service was red.) The Japanese had dispatched authorities to draft Korean workers and had launched an aggressive manhunt, employing Korean civil servants and police. Each township (*myŏn*) was required to supply a certain number of draftees and was allowed to meet its quota by whatever means it cared to employ. If a *myŏn* failed to produce the necessary number of volunteers, it would hunt down and capture men to fill its quota.

I vividly remember these and other raids. In the village where I grew up, the Japanese authorities came and killed all the dogs. A specific recruit called *kae paek chŏng,* meaning "dog butcher," had been designated to catch and kill them. As I recall, the butchering was explained to us as necessary to prevent the dogs from going mad and injuring people when the American planes bombed the village. Others said that the massacre of dogs was a plan to save food, because a dog consumed as much food as a human being. One may, however, also entertain the hypothesis that by killing the dogs the Japanese hoped to eliminate a warning when they raided the villages during their manhunts.

P'il-yŏ and her brother requested Ch'ang-ho's return, but the police told them that nothing could be done. They further inquired about him from the mobilization authorities, but Ch'ang-ho had already been sent from the peninsula and was headed toward Hokkaido, the northern island of Japan. The mobilization authorities assumed that he would arrive in Sakhalin within the next few weeks. No one could do anything about the matter.

A month later P'il-yŏ finally received a letter from Ch'ang-ho, who was in Korsakov on the southern tip of Sakhalin Island; he said that soon he would be working on the construction of an airport runway and would be back home after six months. In the letter he was apologetic to his family about not informing them when he joined the Work Corps.

P'il-yŏ waited for his return. In April 1944, after the long-awaited six months had passed, Ch'ang-ho wrote that his contract had been extended arbitrarily to a full year. It was a great disappointment for the family. Three months later, on August 13, 1944, about a year before the end of the war, P'il-yŏ received a third letter from Ch'ang-ho, in which he indicated that he might be transferred at any time to some area in the South Pacific. The letter was sent from Toyohara (now Yuzhno-Sakhalinsk), the capital of southern Sakhalin. This was Ch'ang-ho's last letter.

I was also interested to know what had happened to P'il-yŏ's husband Ch'il-sŏng, but when I began asking her about him, P'il-yŏ turned away and said she did not want to talk about it any further. Her face turned red, and she lit a cigarette. Even her polite daughter, Sun-ok, did not seem to appreciate my follow-up questions concerning her father. Later, when I asked my sisters and sister-in-law about Ch'il-sŏng, they knew few details about him because this was one of the few subjects that Sun-ok did not want to talk about even with her close friends.

Before the year had passed for Ch'ang-ho's return, the war came to an end. Ch'ang-ho's family hoped that he would return promptly. Many Koreans who had been sent overseas during the war did return home, and Pusan harbor was crowded with the returnees. However, no Koreans who had been taken to Sakhalin came home. P'il-yŏ waited another year, but Ch'ang-ho still did not return. Later she learned that the Koreans who had gone to Sakhalin were trapped there because it was now occupied by Russia, and they were unable to communicate with their relatives in South Korea.

Although Ch'ang-ho had said in his last letter that he might be transferred to the South Pacific, there was no proof that he had actually been transferred. There was a possibility that he was still on Sakhalin Island. However, if he had gone to the Pacific front and had survived, he would have already been repatriated. His failure to return indicated that he might have been killed in action in the Pacific, in which case the Japanese authorities would probably not have informed his family of his death.

P'il-yŏ chose to believe that Ch'ang-ho was still on Sakhalin. However, when the SRDS (the Society for the Return of Detainees on Sakhalin) published a list of Koreans who wished to be repatriated from Sakhalin, his name was not on it. Returnees repatriated via Japan because their spouses were Japanese gave many tragic accounts of Koreans on Sakhalin. Some had been killed in coal mines and in the construction of railroads, harbors, and airports. Others had committed suicide. Many had died from exposure to the extremely cold weather or of disease and malnutrition. Some had obtained Soviet citizenship, giving up on the idea of returning to Korea. Others had obtained North Korean citizenship and had been repatriated to the north. P'il-yŏ does not want to believe that any of these things happened to her son. She trusts that he is still on Sakhalin, is well, and will return to her soon.

In 1947, while she awaited the return of her son, P'il-yŏ arranged a marriage for her daughter, Sun-ok, who was then twenty-one years old. P'il-yŏ's son-in-law is of *yangban* origin but is the son of a secondary wife in a polygynous family. Although he is not well educated, he learned to drive an automobile at a time when not many Koreans were able to drive. He works in Seoul as a cabdriver.

In the meantime, P'il-yŏ and Ch'ang-ho's wife continued to live together, supported mainly by P'il-yŏ's adopted brother. Ch'ang-ho's wife remained loyal to her mother-in-law, despite the absence of her husband. Apparently, however, in late August 1950, in the midst of the Korean War, when P'il-yŏ and her daughter-in-law were separated from her adopted brother's family and were relocated by the North Korean forces, Ch'ang-ho's twenty-seven-year-old wife disappeared.

There is some speculation that P'il-yŏ might have arranged for her young daughter-in-law to go away and start a new life instead of finishing the rest of her life as a semiwidow. Remarriage was difficult, if not forbidden, among *yangban* women, particularly for those whose husbands might still be alive. Because P'il-yŏ and her daughter-in-law had been separated from the other relatives, it was probably believable to say that she had just disappeared. During the war, many North Korean refugees had reconstructed temporary family records in the south. P'il-yŏ's daughter-in-law could have done the same. At any rate, neither my sisters nor my sister-in-law knew any more about her. Since Sun-ok had not been with her mother and sister-in-law, she could not verify this story either. When I asked P'il-yŏ about it, she neither confirmed nor denied what I had been told.

If there are any deceptions in the life history of P'il-yŏ, the story of the disappearance of her daughter-in-law could be one of very few. Clark W. Sorensen has indicated that when information is sought that might reveal deviations from valued cultural norms, such as the chastity of widows, informants seem more likely to give incorrect information.[7]

The chastity and fidelity of women have been strongly mandated since the remote past and are virtues still expected of Korean women. When her husband dies, ideally the wife must remain chaste the rest of her life. Strict chastity and fidelity were demanded even more during the Yi dynasty, according to T'ae-gil Kim, even of a *kisaeng*, or female entertainer.[8]

With the absence of her daughter-in-law from the house, P'il-yŏ experienced such loneliness and emptiness that she could not stay alone. She moved into her adopted brother's home but could not overcome the aching void in her heart. At the strong insistence of Sun-ok and her husband, P'il-yŏ finally joined them in Seoul. She remains there today, helping to rear her grandchildren. Her daughter's family is not affluent, but as her son-in-law has a steady job, they have managed to survive. P'il-yŏ maintains close contact with her adopted brother's home (even though her brother and sister-in-law have passed away) in Ta-dong, hoping that news from her son will eventually arrive there. Ta-dong is the only place from which Ch'ang-ho could trace his family.

Since most of my interviewing was done prior to the reunion telethon, I visited P'il-yŏ again afterward to know what her response to the telethon had been. She and other family members told me that she had watched every touching moment of the program for families who had been separated during the Korean War and was glad to see the good fortune of those who were being reunited. However, apparently she could not help crying as she viewed an eighty-year-old woman desperately seeking her three sons. In her shaking hands the woman held a placard inscribed with the names of her sons who had been missing since the Korean War. Because the old woman knew that she had only fifteen seconds on the program, she was frantically trying to draw the attention of the camera even one more second by lifting her placard as high as possible. She was not allowed to say anything, but her desperation, so apparent on television, was more powerful than any speech could have been.

Having seen the reunion telethon, P'il-yŏ reflected that although there had been some efforts to find family members dispersed during the Korean War, there had been none by either the Japanese or the Koreans to help victims whose family members were taken from them by World War II. "They have been forgotten," she said, holding my hand as I was leaving. I felt helpless, not knowing what to say. She is, of course, not the only one who is awaiting a son's return. Thousands of Korean mothers like P'il-yŏ have been waiting for more than four decades. World War II ended over forty years ago, but peace has not yet come to many Korean women.

CHAPTER 5
Dispersed Spouses

Many married couples became separated because of the Korean War. The histories of a North Korean woman, a South Korean woman, and a North Korean man are presented here as examples of dispersed spouses who continued to remain faithful to their missing partners.

A NORTH KOREAN WOMAN

For my case studies, I wanted to find a representative North Korean woman now living in South Korea who had left her husband in the north during the Korean War. I asked many North Korean refugees about locating such a person, but they told me that it would be difficult. The rarity of such cases is closely related to Korean social norms regulating family and kinship, which require women to follow rather than lead their husbands. The Korean expression "a thread follows wherever a needle leads" is an apt metaphor for the dependency of Korean women on their husbands.

Finally, after a long period of inquiry, a good friend told me that her best friend's sister had fled from the north without her husband, taking their only child. This woman was now living in North America. My friend said, "You can hardly believe her story, but when you hear it, it makes sense how it happened. I have known her for a long time, since her sister is my best friend. I know almost everything about her." My friend was trying to imply that the woman had not deliberately deviated from Korean social norms and was a decent woman. My friend was also willing to be a key informant about the woman.

When I expressed my interest in learning about her friend's sister, my friend invited me to her home for dinner and a chat. My friend's husband was a North Korean refugee who had fled south alone as a young boy, and he had many things to tell me. At the same time, I had much to tell them about their son, who was studying at the university where I was affiliated. During and after dinner, I found that focusing on a specific subject was not easy, because I was interested in asking my friend questions about her friend's sister for my study, but her husband was interested in telling me about his ordeal, including his escape from the north, his hard life in the south, and his final success as a businessman, and my friend was more interested in knowing how her son was doing in an American university. However, my friend said she would arrange for me to meet her friend, so that I could try and get more information about her sister. Parenthetically, Koreans rarely invite guests to their homes unless they are going to serve a formal dinner or have a decent meal for them. Inviting someone to one's home for conversation over a cup of coffee or tea is considered inhospitable. Thus, it was inappropriate for me to ask, even though we were good friends, whether we could all meet at my friend's home for the interviews. Instead, I invited them to come to my hotel coffee shop.

Most of the factual information about my subject was collected through these two key informants, my friend and her friend, the subject's sister. I was fortunate enough to meet my subject, however, during a visit she made to Seoul in the summer of 1983. Her visit proved to be a windfall to my fieldwork equally as important as the reunion telethon. She agreed to let me interview her directly, and at my insistence, to avoid additional hardship on my friend in preparing dinners, we also met in my hotel coffee shop, which was located in the outskirts of Seoul toward the mountains and was generally very quiet during the day.

In-suk Park was born in 1926, the second daughter among the eight sons and daughters of a landlord and businessman, T'ae-ho Park, who was engaged in the textile industry in T'ae-hŭng in Hwanghae-do province in what is now North Korea. Like most local landlords of that day, In-suk's father owned a house in Seoul, which had the best educational facilities in Korea, for the purpose of educating his children. Usually landlords sent their sons to Seoul after they had completed elementary school in their hometowns. It was a privilege hardly ever extended to their daughters, who were kept at home. Education for girls, other than learning domestic skills, has traditionally been overlooked in Korea. Until the proclamation of the secondary school act in 1908, two years before the Japanese annexation of Korea, the government of the Yi dynasty had had nothing to do with women's education at any level, and even under this act secondary education was still only optional for women. Under Japanese colonial rule, the situation did not improve.[1] Since In-suk's father was a conservative Confucianist, In-suk remained at home, where she attended elementary and high schools, while her brothers were studying in Seoul.

In-suk was the most beloved daughter. She had a high "market value" as a bride in the "marriage markets," to use William Goode's terms, since she had beauty, intelligence, family reputation, wealth, charm, and courage.[2] Many matchmakers were interested in arranging her marriage. However, although she was more desirable and attractive as a bride than her older sister, her parents would not allow her to marry before her older sister had married. Traditionally, the order of marriage among Korean siblings concurred with their birth order. This practice has been relaxed, especially if there is an older brother and a younger sister. However, among sisters, it is still highly desirable for the elder sisters to marry before the younger ones. While In-suk was waiting her turn for marriage, she spent her time learning to cook, sew, and do other work that was required of a *hyŏn-mo yang-ch'ŏ* (good wife and wise mother).

When In-suk was nineteen and still preparing for her future role, Korea was liberated from Japan, and the Korean peninsula was subsequently divided along the thirty-eighth parallel. When the Soviet occupation forces arrived in North Korea, her family faced major turmoil and had to cope with the radical changes of the political circumstances. In-suk and her family were cut off from her brothers studying in Seoul, south of the thirty-eighth parallel. Because her father was a rich landlord, her family was subject to discrimination.[3] The pressures and discrimination intensified after the communist government of North Korea was inaugurated in 1948. After the declaration of so-called democratic reform, a revolutionary land-reform decree came into effect. There was a purge of landlords and anticommunist reactionaries. In-suk's family lost all of their land and began actively to seek refuge in South Korea.

It became difficult for a family such as In-suk's to select marriage partners for their offspring, and In-suk's parents almost gave up trying to arrange a marriage for her. In North Korea at that time political background was an "important consideration" in the selection of a spouse. Those who had a "bad element" in their background (children of the exploiting class, collaborators of the Japanese in the past, or relatives of those who fled south) or who were related to a "bad element" could have "a difficult time finding a marriage partner," for this was "an important factor in a person's future career prospects."[4]

In 1948, however, when In-suk turned twenty-two, someone arranged for her to meet a twenty-eight-year-old lawyer named Kwang-dong Kwak from the village of To-dong, not far from her hometown. In North Korea under communist rule, "love match," or free choice, marriages were becoming increasingly common, but go-betweens were still employed, and party members were sometimes asked to arrange meetings between prospective spouses.[5] In-suk and Kwang-dong met at a *mat-sŏn* and became attracted to each other.

Mat-sŏn refers to an arranged meeting between an eligible young man and an unmarried young woman with representatives of their families. It represents a compromise between arranged marriage by the parents and free choice of a mate by a prospective bride or groom. Before the *mat-sŏn* both families discuss the matter thoroughly and quietly investigate each other through friends and, in some cases, private detectives. After the investigations and discussions are favorably concluded, the formal *mat-sŏn* is held. This custom is also popular in Japan, where it is called *miai*.[6]

Kwang-dong was known to be brilliant. He had studied at a prestigious law school in Tokyo and had passed the Japanese civil service examination (*kosi*). This exam was so selective that it was difficult for Japanese to pass it, let alone Koreans, who were subject to discrimination and usually denied equal opportunity with Japanese.[7] Passing the *kosi* was the avenue to practicing law or to becoming appointed a public prosecutor or judge. Before the end of World War II, Kwang-dong had joined a law firm in P'yŏngyang and practiced law there. Upon the liberation of Korea from Japan, he remained in P'yŏngyang and served as a legal consultant for the communist party. Nevertheless, his being the eldest son of a wealthy landlord was a political liability. Like In-suk's family, his family also owned a house in Seoul, and all of his younger brothers were in Seoul for their education. Because she shared many common factors with him, In-suk was an ideal marriage candidate for him.

Many North Koreans who were labeled "bad elements" by the North Korean authorities were the remnants of the well-to-do class. I was never convinced that every North Korean refugee had been rich, even though

I have never met any North Korean refugee who said that he or she was poor and humble in the north. If I had not known that the families of both In-suk and her husband had had houses in Seoul for the education of their children, I would have questioned the claims about their class background rigorously.

Kwang-dong and In-suk were married in 1948. After the wedding In-suk did not stay very long with her parents-in-law. She followed Kwang-dong and moved to P'yŏngyang, where he was working for the party. Despite the political turmoil, they had a happy life without interference from their in-laws. Soon, they had their first child, a boy they named Tong-ha. Although as the oldest son, Kwang-dong was responsible for the care of his parents, he had left them in their home and had established his nuclear family in a separate residence and location. But because his parents were still active, this was a permissible, if somewhat unorthodox, arrangement.

Because of the external political pressures, In-suk and her husband had thought about fleeing south. But crossing the thirty-eighth parallel, even with the help of paid guides, was dangerous. They had hesitated to undertake such a risky venture during In-suk's pregnancy. Then, once she had the baby, it became even harder to take such a risk. The couple were also fearful of possible repercussions for their families if they fled south. As they continued to deliberate, the guard at the border became tighter than ever, making it virtually impossible for them to make such a bold move. Moreover, In-suk became pregnant again; she was expecting her second child when the Korean War began.

In the early stages of the war Kwang-dong and In-suk thought that there would be no contest when they learned that almost all of the south was occupied by North Korean forces. They worried about the safety of their brothers in Seoul. If they had fled and been caught in the south by the northern occupation forces, they would have faced serious punishment. But the war did not proceed as the northern leaders hoped. It took a radical turn in favor of the United Nations forces when General MacArthur made his spectacular landing at Inch'ŏn. After the United Nations forces marched northward and crossed the thirty-eighth parallel, In-suk and her son, Tong-ha, went to the house of her parents-in-law in Ta-dong, where she could give birth to her second child. Because Ta-dong was a smaller city than P'yŏngyang, it was less vulnerable to bombings. In the meantime, her husband stayed in P'yŏngyang alone.

In late fall 1950, while In-suk was in Ta-dong with her parents-in-law, her husband's brother Kwang-jun, a captain of the South Korean army medical corps, arrived home. He was part of the United Nations and South Korean military forces that were pushing northward. It was In-suk's first meeting with her brother-in-law. About that time, In-suk also heard that her two brothers who had stayed in Seoul had come to their natal home in T'ae-hǔng as officers of the South Korean army. As did most North Koreans, In-suk now thought that the war would soon be over, that the divided country would be unified, and that separated families would be reunited. But suddenly in late November Kwang-jun came to ask his parents and sister-in-law to leave immediately for the south. He told them that the involvement of Chinese communist troops would escalate the war and that the United Nations and South Korean forces were preparing to retreat south. His parents and sister-in-law were reluctant to go to Seoul without Kwang-dong, but Kwang-jun warned them that they had little time to consider and that they must leave immediately. In-suk's parents-in-law were ready to flee, but she wanted to go to P'yŏngyang to find her husband. Kwang-jun promised his sister-in-law that he would make every effort to find his brother in P'yŏngyang and make arrangements for him to join them in their Seoul home, but In-suk adamantly refused to go along with the idea.

I was unable to find out why Kwang-dong had stayed in P'yŏngyang instead of coming home to join his wife, son, and parents while the northern troops were retreating from P'yŏngyang as the United Nations and South Korean forces were approaching. He might have been afraid of facing the United Nations and South Korean forces. As mentioned elsewhere, this is, however, a most sensitive question and one difficult to answer honestly. My friend speculated that Kwang-dong might have held an important post for the party, which I was unable to prove or disprove.

Word came from In-suk's own parents in T'ae-hǔng that they had decided to go to Seoul at the insistence of their two sons. They strongly encouraged In-suk to go south too. In-suk's father-in-law insisted that he be allowed to take his two-year-old grandson, Tong-ha, with him to the south if In-suk decided to stay in North Korea. Tong-ha was his eldest grandson (*chongson*) and thus the main heir of his family and lineage (*munjung*). (In Korea the head of the *munjung* is also called the *chongson*, and he is the patriline successor, which is usually the eldest male descendent of the ancestor. The *chongson* leads meetings and the ancestral worship services of the *munjung*. He is usually assisted and counseled by elders of the oldest generations.)[8] For In-suk, it was as unthinkable to be separated from Tong-ha as from her husband. Finally, trusting her brother-in-law to make every possible arrangement for her husband, In-suk agreed to follow her parents-in-law. In late November of 1950 they left Ta-dong.

In-suk's journey south was not as arduous as it had been for others even though she was pregnant. She was well taken care of by her parents-in-law during her relocation, and they had started well ahead of the ever-increasing crowd of fleeing refugees. Once in Seoul, In-suk did not suffer from the problems of adjusting to an alien city as much as other refugees did. All of her family except her husband was with her. Her parents lived a short distance from her residence with her in-laws. In-suk and her family were comfortable in their already established Seoul home, whereas other refugees had to stay in the temporary shelters of refugee camps and suffered from hunger and cold during the winter months. Because of insufficient relief funds, there was a lack of manpower and facilities, and the camps were severely overcrowded.

In-suk expected her husband to arrive any day. Hundreds of thousands of North Korean refugees were coming south, but Kwang-dong was not among them. Had he fled south, Kwang-dong would not have had any difficulty finding his family because he knew Seoul well and knew also that his family would return to their house there. (Kwang-dong had lived in the house while attending secondary school before he went to Tokyo for his college education.) Sometime after the birth of her second son, Tong-jin, In-suk was told by her brother-in-law, Kwang-jun, that he had been unable to locate his brother in P'yŏngyang and that he believed that the communist party leaders there had taken Kwang-dong northward with them.

Unlike many women who had little children and who were separated from their husbands and other relatives, In-suk had the support of her natal family and of the family of her husband. But rearing two sons without her husband was not easy, and her hopes for reunion with her husband were soon shattered. The major northward offensive by the United Nations forces never happened; instead, the war became deadlocked, and the front lines were stalled near the thirty-eighth parallel. On July 27, 1953, a ceasefire was declared, truce lines were drawn, and the division of the country was reaffirmed. So long as Korea was divided, In-suk and her two sons would never be able to see Kwang-dong, her husband and their father.

The financial situation of In-suk's family in Seoul worsened. The large number of family members, which included In-suk's parents-in-law, her unmarried brothers- and sisters-in-law, and In-suk and her two sons, were unable to continue living off one income. Kwang-jun's salary as an army officer was not sufficient to feed all of them, and In-suk's father-in-law was incapable of working. He was a landlord who had inherited wealth from his parents and had never made any money on his own. He had no marketable skills nor any formal education. In-suk began to realize that if their situation continued much longer she would be unable to feed her children or provide for their education. She had to do something other than think sadly about her distant husband and the happy days of her past.

Her father-in-law was incompetent in financial management, but her own father, T'ae-ho, was a capable businessman. Since relocating to Seoul, he had started several businesses from nothing and was managing them successfully. He owned several stores in the Tongdae-mun and Namdae-mun markets. In-suk asked his help to start a business to assist her husband's family.

She had a tea room (*tabang*) in mind. During and after the war, tea rooms in Korea were used for several purposes: for meeting friends, for conducting business transactions, and for general socializing and even flirting. In those war-torn days not many people could maintain a decent house with a living room to entertain guests and friends, nor could small businesspeople find offices. Most people and businesses could not afford telephones. Tea rooms were easy to identify as meeting places, and they usually had telephones for calling in and out. Most important, the facilities could be used very inexpensively; one had only to buy a cup of coffee or tea to be able to stay for several hours. Because of such social demand, tea rooms were everywhere and were considered a lucrative service business for a woman to run. They were owned and operated mostly by single women and widows created by the war. However, a social stigma was attached to women who managed tea rooms; respectable women did not even go into them. Because of this negative image, In-suk's father strongly opposed her business plan. Instead, he set up a cosmetics shop for her.

In-suk became skillful in running her business and did well. She concluded, however, that the cosmetics shop was not profitable enough. Despite her father's objections, she also opened a tea room and hired another woman to run it.

She worked hard to keep her mind off her troubles, and finally she earned enough money to become financially independent and purchase a modest home of her own. She then arranged for her brother-in-law Kwang-jun to take care of her parents-in-law, and she took care of another brother-in-law and one of her sisters-in-law, even paying their university expenses. They also moved into In-suk's home and lived with her. She related that "the main reason for such an arrangement was to eliminate possible rumors. If I had lived alone with my two young children, people might think that I would be interested in having affairs with someone. More than anyone else, I had to convince my father. Besides, if I had just left them on their own, my brother-in-law and sister-in-law probably would not have had a chance to pursue their college educations. I wanted to help them."

No matter what she did nor how hard she worked, it was not easy for her to overcome the loneliness of being single. No words can describe the struggles of her lonely life. She was twenty-four years old, an age at which some women had not yet even married. "The most difficult problem was handling the sympathy from others," In-suk said shyly, "especially from men. They thought that I could not go on alone."

According to my friend, many men were genuinely interested in In-suk because she was still young, attractive, and a capable person. However, others were attracted to her because she was financially independent. In-suk's father kept reminding her that "you have to stay away from men, because they are only interested in you because you are a capable woman financially."

According to In-suk's older sister, one man who had fled south alone from the same city from which In-suk had fled became very interested in her and proposed marriage to her several times. He was a decent man and even appealed directly to In-suk's father for his permission. But In-suk remained faithful to her husband. She was a chaste woman, and she made every effort to preserve her virtue.

In-suk's sister speculated that the presence of so many of her kin in Seoul, both her own and her husband's, discouraged In-suk from thinking of remarrying. In-suk's sister particularly blamed their father. "If my father had not insisted that In-suk remain single, who knows, she might have married. I'm proud of her for being so faithful to her husband, her sons, and her relatives, but what has she accomplished other than having a painful and tortured life?" My impression was that In-suk was neither proud nor regretful of what she had done and she certainly did not blame her father, now deceased.

In-suk was grateful for her two sons, who were healthy and did well in school. Both graduated from prestigious universities in Seoul, and one completed graduate school, receiving his master's degree. In the meantime, four of In-suk's brothers-in-law and sisters-in-law, including the two who had lived with her, settled in the United States and Canada, having found good jobs. The brother-in-law and sister-in-law who had been supported and educated by In-suk wished to return the favor, and so they invited In-suk and her sons to live in the United States. They were especially thankful for In-suk's dedication in rearing their nephews Tong-jin and particularly Tong-ha, who was their *chongson*, or main heir of their lineage. They wished to gather their kin together again in the alien land of North America.

In-suk was ambivalent. She was reluctant to leave her Korean homeland, but it had also become loathsome to her as the place where she had been separated from her husband because of the war. She certainly did not want such a tragedy to happen to her descendants, who would be vulnerable as long as they remained in Korea. She had some fears about emigrating to a foreign country, but at the same time Seoul was not her hometown. At the insistence of her two sons, she finally agreed to go with them to America. In 1973, after selling all her assets in Seoul, she followed her sons to a new world.

By remaining faithful to her husband, she had met the ethical standards of the chaste woman. By following her sons, she was upholding one of the strongest moral codes required of an upper-class woman under Confucianism, the three rules of obedience (*samjong chido*), which required that a woman follow her parents in youth, her husband in marriage, and her sons in old age. In-suk, of course, had followed her parents during her childhood and adolescence, and now she was going to follow her sons. But she wondered how she would be regarded for not having followed her husband, even though the war had prevented her from fulfilling this *samjong chido*. She seemed to think that she should have gone to her husband and remained with him no matter what had happened.

In-suk is now fifty-eight years old (in 1983). Her two sons are thirty-six and thirty-four. She presently has three grandchildren. She lives with Tong-ha, her oldest son, in America, and her second son lives nearby. She enjoys playing with and taking care of her grandchildren. Her life in America is good, comfortable, and safe from the threat of war. But her daily life is not always easy or convenient. "I cannot speak any English and cannot drive," she said, "I feel like a handicapped person. Soon, I won't even be able to communicate with my grandchildren, because they speak more English as they grow older." Although her sons and daughters-in-law are doing the best they can for her, they cannot eliminate her loneliness, her longing for her husband. Every other year In-suk visits Seoul to see her sister and friends.

People tell her that she might be able to visit North Korea to find her husband. But she does not believe such a visit is possible. An increasing number of Korean-Americans and Korean-Canadians have visited and been reunited with their family members in China, mostly in the Korean Autonomous Prefecture of Jilin province, and have invited them to the United States and Canada. But few Korean-Americans or Korean-Canadians have been able to get into North Korea. A free-lance journalist and Korean-American, Peter Hyun, visited North Korea in 1976 to report for Harper's Magazine Press and CBS-TV. He was able to locate his father's grave but was unable to document other accounts he had in mind, for example, on the lives of contemporary North Koreans.[9] In 1981 a group of six Korean-American political scientists visited North Korea upon the invitation of the North Korean government, but their trip was not for a family reunion.[10]

No one knows if North Korea will ever allow South Koreans or even overseas Korean residents to search for family members separated from them during the Korean War. Even if it does, I do not know if In-suk would try to seek her separated husband. Her visit could jeopardize Kwang-dong's safety and well-being and could also disrupt his family life if he has remarried.

A SOUTH KOREAN WOMAN

Quite different are the many cases of South Korean women who remained in the south while their husbands went voluntarily or involuntarily to North Korea. Leaving behind their spouses and other family members, South Korean communists and their sympathizers fled north, and an estimated 85,000 South Koreans, mostly political leaders, reputable scholars, intellectuals, and writers, were kidnapped and taken north by the North Korean authorities during the three-month period from June 25 to September 15, 1950. Because the issue has been and is still politically sensitive, people do not want to reveal their knowledge of or discuss relatives who voluntarily went north. Thus I selected as a case study the wife of a kidnapped South Korean.

Hi-suk Kim is a distant relative. We were very close, however, and I considered her almost like a big sister, particularly during her years of struggle in Seoul, when I often visited her apartment. I feel I can probably be a better informant about her life than most others. Also, because of our relationship, during my fieldwork I was able to freely stop by where she now lives and ask almost any question.

Hi-suk was born into a *yangban* family in Kyo-dong, a small rural town in a southeastern province, the only daughter among three children. Her grandfather was a typical Confucian scholar, but he had recognized the importance and benefits of modern education for his children and for his country. He had been able to send his three sons to university in Japan. Two of them found good jobs in the Japanese colonial government upon the completion of their education, but Su-nam Kim, Hi-suk's father, refused to work for the Japanese. Instead, he participated in the underground anti-Japanese independence movement.

Because of his strong anti-Japanese stand, Su-nam had even refused to change his name and the names of his children according to Japanese style when almost all Koreans had been persuaded to do so. Immediately after the beginning of the Sino-Japanese War in 1937, the conditions of wartime led to the Japanese mobilization of Korea on all fronts—social, political, cultural—and with this began the *naesŏn ilch'ae,* the so-called unification of Japan and Korea. As part of this movement, "Koreans were forcibly encouraged to alter their names, giving them a Japanese style, or were even required to discard completely their traditional names. By September 1940, eighty percent of the total population, that is 16,000,000 persons, had changed their names."[11] Hi-suk was penalized in school because of her Korean-style name, even though she had not been enrolled in Japanese-run schools. She had attended private schools from elementary level to college.

When Korea was liberated from Japan in 1945, Su-nam joined in forming a conservative party and played a leading role in its taking a strong anticommunist stand.

When the Korean War broke out, Su-nam's family, including Hi-suk, tried to persuade him to seek refuge further south. They knew he would be a likely target of the invading communists because of his strong anti-communism and his position in a right-wing party, but Su-nam refused to flee, trusting that governmental officials would not abandon their citizens. Hi-suk recalled him saying, "I cannot leave other people behind and run away by myself just because as a privileged person I had information earlier than they." He could not believe that the president would slip away from the city without telling his people, but the Han River Bridge was destroyed soon after the presidential parties crossed it. The government's plan backfired, for it trapped its own military forces and civilians in the city.

Su-nam also trusted in the ability of the South Korean military forces; he believed that the enemy invasion of Seoul would be temporary, that the South Korean army would regroup and recapture the capital city, and that everything would return to normal. He planned to hide temporarily, if necessary, and he even persuaded Hi-suk and her family not to flee south. He told Hi-suk, "Tell your husband to stay home, not to go outside. It will be all right after a few days, if not in a few weeks." Added to his strong principles, Su-nam's optimism led to his being kidnapped by the northern authorities on a muggy day in early July 1950.

Su-nam's kidnapping could have been prevented or avoided if the true situation in the early stages of the war had been revealed to the populace. From the very beginning of the Korean War, the South Korean military forces were unable to check the rapid advance of the northern forces on all fronts, mainly because of poor equipment and inferior manpower. Although he was a prominent politician, Su-nam was not informed of the government's plan to evacuate south over the Han River until the early session of an emergency cabinet meeting held at 2:00 A.M., June 27, 1950. By then the North Korean forces had reached the outskirts of Seoul, and the next day, to block their southward advance, the South Korean Army Corps of Engineers blew up the Han River Bridge. There was not sufficient time for an orderly evacuation, and the government continued to broadcast the message that Seoul would be protected from enemy attack and that citizens should remain calm.

Hi-suk's husband, Ch'angbae Choi, was a researcher and an instructor at a college in Seoul. Marriage between Hi-suk and Ch'ang-bae had been arranged. Their family backgrounds were almost identical: both were of *yangban* origin and landowner backgrounds; both of their fathers were the first generation of the family to attend college; and their mothers had had no formal education.

After North Korea invaded Seoul, Ch'ang-bae, taking his father-in-law's advice, hid in the basement of his house and would not see anyone. However, in mid-July, a student came by looking for Ch'ang-bae. The student was no stranger; he had been in Ch'ang-bae's and Hi-suk's home before, and Hi-suk had met him. Because Ch'ang-bae and Hi-suk trusted him, Ch'ang-bae agreed to meet the student without knowing that he was an agent of the communists. After the student's visit Ch'ang-bae was forced to participate in recruiting college students for the Student Army Corps. Suddenly, at the end of July, however, despite Ch'ang-bae's cooperation, two plainclothes North Korean agents arrested him. Hi-suk never saw her husband again. Under custody of the North Korean authorities, he was taken to North Korea in the same manner his father-in-law had been taken.

All Koreans were affected by the war, but Hi-suk suffered and endured more than most. After the kidnappings her mother died of severe shock. Her grandfather in Kyo-dong committed suicide during the northern invasion of the village in order to escape the persistent harrassment of the communists for being a landlord and the father of a prominent South Korean politician. Her younger brother drowned while crossing the river on his way from Seoul to Kyo-dong to seek refuge in his hometown. She had reached a breaking point and could not take any more. Taking her one-year-old son Pong-guk with her, she moved to T'ap-ri to live with her parents-in-law.

Because Hi-suk had grown up in Seoul after her father had settled there upon his return from Japan, she was unaccustomed to the rural life of T'ap-ri, even though her roots were in a rural village. Her four years in T'ap-ri were not easy, although her hardships were not altogether associated with her husband's absence and her having to rear her son alone. Many of her difficulties stemmed from the family structure and system that was typical of a *yangban* family heavily influenced by Confucianism. Hi-suk's life was not always comfortable, with so many family members present: her brother-in-law and his wife and three children also lived with her in-laws.

Preparing the regular meals for the family was difficult enough, considering how large it was, but worse than that was preparing the special meals for their ancestors on the anniversaries of their deaths. The family was the main heir of the lineage, and it had to observe ancestor worship rites often, honoring all dead ancestors for five generations. Because she was unaccustomed to hard work, the responsibility of preparing for the ancestors' rituals often made Hi-suk ill. (A Korean proverb expresses the attitude of the Korean mother-in-law: "The good-for-nothing daughter-in-law gets sick on the day of ancestral sacrifice."[12]) Hi-suk's mother-in-law, who was reputed to be hard to get along with, did not particularly like her daughter-in-law.

The family had been prosperous landowners when Hi-suk and Ch'ang-bae married. But in the land reform of Syngman Rhee's administration just before the Korean War, the family had lost most of its land except for limited acreage nearby that was unable to support so many people. Their financial situation continued to deteriorate as Hi-suk's brother-in-law lost a congressional race, and the debts stemming from his campaign mounted. Hi-suk realized that if matters were left to her brother-in-law, the financial condition of the family would worsen, and its assets would probably end up being mortgaged to pay for his unsuccessful political campaign. If that happened, Hi-suk worried that she would not be able to educate her son adequately.

When the war ended, Hi-suk began to have serious discussions with her father-in-law about her and her son's future, despite the objections and nagging of her mother-in-law. She wanted to receive her share of the family assets to go back to Seoul, where she could ensure that Pong-guk would get a good education. She insisted that Pong-guk was the *chongson*, the main heir of his lineage, and that his education was important.

At first, Hi-suk's father-in-law adamantly denied the request of his rebellious daughter-in-law. After some time, however, she persuaded him and he acceded. He sold some of the leftover land and provided cash for her to settle in Seoul, even though her mother-in-law and her brother-in-law believed that the family was merely providing money for Hi-suk to have an easy life in the city.

Her four years in T'ap-ri had seemed like an eternity to Hi-suk. She was only twenty-eight, but hardship, loneliness, and country life had made her look older. Nevertheless, she could have remarried if she had so desired, but instead she chose to remain faithful to her husband.

Hi-suk's relocation to Seoul with a five-year-old son, however, was not an easy one at all. Raising a child alone was difficult, and even being dependent on her in-laws was a burden, since she did not have any steady source of income until she had a job in the late 1960s. Without knowing anything of her struggle, I often stopped by her apartment and had meals. Sometimes, I brought my friends with me. Because she was living in a modern apartment (which was unusual then), I as a high school student thought she was very rich.

During the late 1960s and early 1970s, because of the postwar economic recovery in Seoul and the expansion of Japanese business in Korea after the signing of the normalization treaty in 1965, many Japanese firms in Seoul needed Korean employees who could act as interpreters. Because she could speak Japanese and also had a two-year college degree, Hi-suk was able to get a job with a Japanese company. Her income was steady, and by the time her son entered college, it was sizable.

Pong-guk graduated from the elite business school of a prestigious university in the early 1970s. He was recruited by a leading Korean company that had offices throughout the world at a time when many ambitious young Korean entrepreneurs were starting to exploit world markets. Recognizing Pong-guk's ability, the company soon promoted him to a good position. He became chief officer of its Hong-Kong branch, where he was in charge of the business's operations in several southeastern countries.

Pong-guk had become an extremely eligible marriage candidate and was in a commanding position to select a qualified candidate to be his bride. His value was high, not only because he had graduated from a good school and had a promising future but also because he was of *yangban* origin. The former political position of his maternal grandfather was also taken into account in consideration of his value as a husband. Above all, his mother's faithfulness to his kidnapped father was an advantage for Pong-guk in the marriage market. A friend and relative of Hi-suk recommended her second cousin for Pong-guk. She was of *yangban* origin, a graduate of one of the best women's colleges, and from the same province where Pong-guk was from. "Certainly, a decent family considers it important that I have remained single," said Hi-suk. "But, I am not so sure that it is worthwhile for a woman to sacrifice her chance of remarrying just to enhance her selection of a good daughter-in-law. I never calculated that it would be an advantage for my son."

Now (in 1983) a thirty-six-year-old businessman, Pong-guk lives with his wife and two sons overseas. Fifty-eight-year-old Hi-suk lives alone in a small apartment on the outskirts of Seoul. With Pong-guk's support, she no longer has to work for a living. She does volunteer work for various charity organizations and spends time visiting friends and relatives. Every now and then she visits her son and his family wherever he has been posted. She has been to Hong Kong, Manila, and other major cities. Still, Hi-suk spends much of her time in her lonely apartment in Seoul thinking about her past: "If I told you I no longer think about my husband, I would be telling you a lie. In T'ap-ri I often directed my anger against my in-laws so that I could forget my longing for him. And, until Pong-guk was able to be on his own, I really did not have the luxury of being melancholy. I was too busy earning a living. I did not have time to worry about other things. Now, I think about my husband more than ever before. I hope that he has remarried and has his own family, so that he does not feel the aching pain of loneliness that I do."

I asked Hi-suk, "If your husband has remarried and has a family, what will you do if reunions between dispersed family members in the north and south become possible?" She could only give a sigh as an answer.

A NORTH KOREAN MAN

Koreans believe that women can remain single much more easily than men. An old Korean proverb reflects this sentiment: "The widower has three measures of lice while the widow has three measures of rice"; a man cannot live alone, but a woman somehow knows how to manage without her husband.[13] Because few North Korean women went south without their husbands, single men outnumbered single women among North Korean refugees, although the exact ratio has never been calculated. Few North Korean men have remained single since their relocation, and those that have have been considered unusual and even extraordinary. The Korean media have treated such cases as exceptional and reported them widely.

I identified two North Korean men who had remained single since the end of the war, both of whom had appeared in the media. Ki-su Kim was dispersed from his wife during World War II, when he was smuggled into Manchuria to evade the Japanese military draft. He had been single for nearly forty years when, finally, in 1978 he wrote a letter to his home address with the names of multiple recipients. With the help of the South Korean Red Cross, it was delivered to his son. Ironically, when Ki-su had slipped away from his home in 1943 to avoid the Japanese authorities, he had been unaware of the pregnancy of his wife. In 1981, when he returned from Manchuria after nearly four decades, he was given a heroic welcome. His reunion with his wife (who had not remarried) and family was wonderful, and no one blamed him for staying in Manchuria after the war was over and ignoring his family in Korea. The Korean media failed to comment on his irresponsibility as a husband, choosing instead to lionize his lengthy chastity. My friends and informants have been unable to grasp my more critical view of him.

I decided to document the history of the other man, Tong-hi Lee, for this work. Since he had also become a celebrity because of having remained single for all those years, part of his personal story had already become public knowledge. Before I undertook this study or had interviewed him, I had read Tong-hi's autobiography and essays written about him so I was somewhat acquainted with him. Even though he is widely known in Korea, I have tried to conceal his identity for the reasons I have mentioned previously.

Tong-hi was a busy man. He had a tight schedule and was often out of town. An American-educated sociologist and a good friend of mine at a university in Pusan made the arrangements for my interview with him. Most of my interviews with Tong-hi took place in his office inside the hospital that he had established in Pusan. The office was humble, but cozy enough to conduct an interview, and once he went in there no one dared bother him. The hospital staff believed that if he was not engaged in an important matter, he would be available for his patients, nurses, and other staff members. I had noticed that the hospital staff yielded to him or stayed away from his side when he was walking in the hallway, expressing their respect for him.

Before I started the interview on the first day, I tried to explain the purpose of my study, how it would be conducted, and how it would be treated after the project was completed. He interrupted me and said, "You don't have to repeat your introduction. I heard about you and your project from your friend. I'd like to help you anyway I can for a good cause." His one concern was how long the interview would take. He then asked me to pray with him before the interview. In his prayer, he wished that the good Lord would give me strength and wisdom in documenting the tragedy of family dispersal and in revealing its inhumanity to all human races on earth. I was touched by his brief words of prayer, which gave me a sense of destiny as an anthropologist in doing this project. I have never met such an informant in my professional career.

Tong-hi Lee is a seventy-three-year-old physician (in 1983). He was born in 1911, one year after the annexation of Korea to Japan, in Yongchŏng-ri, a farming town in P'yŏngan Nam-do province in North Korea. His stated birth date differs from the one recorded in the official census register (*hojŏk*) compiled by the Japanese colonial government, in which, according to the official census, his birth year is listed as 1909. When the Japanese authorities were taking a census, Tong-hi's uncle misinformed them about the birth year of his nephew because he was worried that they would raise the legal age of marriage for Koreans. The uncle wanted his nephew to marry early as was customary at that time. Unlike the Anglo-American legal tradition, Japanese and Korean civil codes recognize the birth date and year as they are registered, regardless of the date of the actual event.

When he was born, Tong-hi's family was comfortable financially. His grandfather was not a landlord himself but was a supervisor of tenant farmers for several absentee landlords in Seoul who owned large farms. Utilizing his role as a tenant supervisor, he was able to accumulate enough wealth to purchase his own land. The size of this farmland grew as time went on.

Although Tong-hi's grandfather was conservative in fiscal matters, his father was very liberal. His father was an entrepreneur, mostly in real estate, and had invested heavily in land in Seoul and Manchuria. He was not a successful businessman, however, and his investments usually resulted in great losses. Nevertheless, he never hesitated to invest and to spend more money. But he was not at all a good-for-nothing. He was interested in modern education and established a five-year elementary school near his village. (At that time, Chinese classics taught by Confucian tutors was considered the proper education for Korean youths.) This modern school provided a unique opportunity for the youngsters of the village.

Tong-hi's childhood seems to have been comfortable and enjoyable. His father began teaching him Chinese characters in his preschool years but wanted Tong-hi to have a formal education. When Tong-hi was seven years old, his father put him in the school that he had established. Tong-hi's mother was more interested in the development of proper behavior by her son. Tong-hi remembers that his mother, who was a strong disciplinarian, did not hesitate to spank him whenever she considered it necessary. He considers his grandmother, who was a Christian, to have been the most influential person on his career. Until he was seven and ready to go to school, he spent most of his time with her, sleeping in her room and praying with her every morning and evening. Because of his grandmother's impact on him, Tong-hi became a Christian.

Upon graduating from elementary school, he entered a respected high school in Kaesŏng. At first he wanted to become a teacher. Then he thought that he should become an engineer to contribute more to society. When he was about ready to graduate from high school, he decided to become a physician. His choice was primarily in response to the bad financial state of his family; his father's investments in real estate had failed. But he also felt that as a physician he could make a strong contribution to society.

He searched for the least expensive college and enrolled in the state-supported medical school in Seoul, whose tuition was about one-third that of other colleges. Partially supported by his father and staying at his cousin's home in Seoul where he had free room and board, he was able to pursue his medical studies.

Throughout all his school years, including college, Tong-hi had always seemed more religious and conscientious than other students his age. His altruistic commitment was strong, the destiny he saw for himself was clear, and his efforts in his studies were sincere. He did not seem to enjoy extracurricular activities and spent most of his time studying. In medical school he had wanted to play soccer, but he was not good enough to make the team. He went only once to a movie theater during his four years of college in Seoul.

He had been shy during his adolescence, especially with girls. In his senior year in high school, he recalled, he was attracted to a girl in his grade who starred in the school's drama productions, but he was unable to say even a single word to her. Toward the end of his medical school studies, friends and relatives recommended women to him, but he was never really serious about them. His cousin, with whom he was staying in Seoul, wanted to introduce him to a bright woman college student who was from Tong-hi's home province of P'yŏngan Puk-do. But Tong-hi refused even to meet her, thinking she was overqualified for him. He was critical of himself and his financially ailing family, saying, "I could not think of anything I had that was better than what she had, including the wealth of my family, appearance, and other considerations."

As Tong-hi mentioned her name, I realized that I knew the woman well. She had been one of my professors in Seoul and had become the mother-in-law of a good friend of mine. Since retirement as a university professor, she had been serving for a volunteer relief organization. I had gone twice with her in her car to Yŏido Square, where the reunion telethon was taking place, when she was directing assistance for the reunion seekers. She is a widow and has remained single since I first met her in 1957. Had the mood of our interview been more informal, I might have mentioned to Tong-hi what a small world it was.

After he graduated from medical school, Tong-hi's marriage was arranged by one of his classmates. His bridal candidate, Sun-im Park, had only a high school education in P'yŏngyang. When she was introduced to Tong-hi, she was in Seoul with her father, who was working on his dissertation for a doctoral degree in medicine. (The Korean medical school system distinguishes between "doctors" and "physicians." To become a physician, two years of premedical studies and four years of intensive training in medicine are required. If a physician wants to become a doctor, he or she has to study further and prepare a doctoral dissertation.)

Tong-hi said that when he first met Sun-im he "was not particularly impressed or attracted by her." He also realized that "she probably thought of me the same way. Without considering how I looked or who I was, I guess then I was thinking about meeting an exceptional woman." But when his matchmaker friend asked Tong-hi what he thought about the bridal candidate, he replied, "I guess she's all right." His friend interpreted that statement as a sign of positive acceptance and badgered Tong-hi from that time on to make a decision about marriage.

Eventually Tong-hi was persuaded, and he wrote a letter of proposal to Sun-im, asking her to marry him. In his proposal he included three conditions for marriage: she had to convert to Christianity as soon as they were married; they were to live together with his parents and take care of them; and she must be able to work and support them while he was still in medical school as an intern. She accepted his conditions, and they became engaged on March 20. Their wedding took place soon after on April 9, 1932.

Tong-hi's father sold his last acreage in Seoul to pay for the wedding and the expenses of establishing a household for Tong-hi and his bride. But the money from the land was not enough. As an intern with a less-than-adequate paycheck, Tong-hi was still no better off than when he had been a student. He and his new bride, Sun-im, lived with her parents for a year, until her parents returned to P'yŏngyang, where her father practiced medicine.

Tong-hi was promoted to a full-time instructor, and his salary nearly quadrupled. His parents left their home in Yongchŏng-ri and came to live with him and Sun-im in Seoul. The new arrangement was not the best one, for Tong-hi's mother was jealous of her daughter-in-law. At times there were domestic squabbles, and Tong-hi was obliged to take his mother's side. He could do nothing but pray for guidance.

He was dissatisfied with his teaching position at the medical school. He wanted to help poor patients as he had committed himself to do in his youth. In 1940, in spite of having many good job offers and in the face of efforts by his teachers and colleagues to persuade him not to leave Seoul, he went to P'yŏngyang to work in a Christian hospital. During his tenure, he often paid the medical bills for patients who were unable to pay. He frequently bought blood for his patients using his own money. Because of his charity, his family's finances were in poor condition most of the time. His wife had to work part-time washing hospital gowns and sewing hospital uniforms to alleviate their never-ending financial strain.

After the liberation of Korea from Japan, and as North Korea was going under the control of the communists, most of Tong-hi's former teachers and colleagues expected him to return to Seoul. One of his former teachers at the medical school was so certain that Tong-hi would come back that he even provided a teaching position for him. But Tong-hi did not leave P'yŏngyang.

His reasons for staying are complicated. Toward the end of World War II, he began suffering from severe bouts of insomnia. He could not explain why he felt such strong fear and stress, but somehow he could not sleep for weeks. He also suffered from jaundice, and although his jaundiced condition was soon cured, Tong-hi was unable to free himself from stress, and he continued to suffer. Finally, he experienced nervous prostration and could not continue to work. He took sick leave from the hospital and went to a remote hot springs retreat in the mountains to rest himself physically and mentally. While he was recuperating from his malady in the mountain retreat, he heard the news of the Japanese surrender.

He came back recovered to P'yŏngyang in November 1945. He was appointed director and chief of the surgical department of the First People's Hospital there. "In those days we handled more dead bodies than sick patients, because all kinds of terrorists were killing each other in the chaos of the power vacuum," he remembers. "I was about ready to resign from my post in January 1946, when they assigned me additional duties as chief lecturer in the surgical unit of a medical school in a university," he said. "Of course, in that society you cannot resign as you please." He refused to accept the appointment, telling the university officials that he was not qualified to take a professorship, that he was "not fully aware of Marxist ideology, which was essential for a scientist serving in a communist society," and that as a Christian, he could not "work on Sundays" as the joint appointment required him to do.

But the university officials and the officials of the communist party interpreted the first two excuses as personal modesty and simply arranged to meet the third condition. With the promise that he would not be made to work on Sundays, he finally accepted the appointment. He attended church on Sundays without working, and he continued to pray before he operated on patients. The North Korean authorities valued Tong-hi's medical skill and knowledge so highly that they had granted him these unusual privileges.

The North Korean authorities continued to promote Tong-hi. In 1948 they honored him with a model worker's award, with a special pay raise and a doctoral degree. The northern authorities did everything they could to please Tong-hi and assigned him many responsibilities to detain him in the north.

Tong-hi's income in the north was never adequate. Before he had begun receiving preferential treatment, he had had to sell some of his household belongings to meet the needs of his tight budget. In 1948 Sun-im began working for the hospital, making uniforms. Despite awards and preferential treatment, his salary, high by North Korean standards, was still insufficient to support the ten members of his family. But financial restraints were not Tong-hi's primary concern; he had endured financial difficulties most of his life. He was suffering spiritually from limited religious freedom.

Religious freedom was a problem not only for Tong-hi, but also for his firstborn son, Hyŏn-su, who had been born in 1933, a year after Tong-hi and Sun-im's marriage. When Hyŏn-su was in middle school, the school often called students on Sundays and required them to attend various political functions. Because of his strong religious convictions, Hyŏn-su withdrew from the school several weeks just before his graduation. He later attended a vocational night school for training in pharmacology and obtained a license as a parapharmacologist. He worked in a party-run pharmacy until the Korean War began. He was seventeen when he was drafted as a second lieutenant in the medical squad of the North Korean army. His departure for military service was the last farewell between Hyŏn-su and his father.

During the war, Tong-hi was busy treating wounded North Korean soldiers in the university hospital in P'yŏngyang. When the United Nations forces launched northward, he heard that the northern army was retreating. He was told that he would be relocated to a safe place, but when the South Korean and the United Nations forces were about to capture P'yŏngyang, officials of the North Korean government, the party, and the university fled without telling Tong-hi. He did not seek refuge but met the South Korean army in P'yŏngyang. Medical officers of the South Korean army knew who he was and respected him. They asked him to join them in treating wounded soldiers. The South Korean army medical squad provided rice and other necessities for Tong-hi's family. In the meantime, he worked with the South Korean officers in an army field hospital. Tong-hi's work with the South Koreans, however, did not last very long. With the entry into the war of the Chinese People's Volunteers (CPV) in the late fall of 1950, the war turned in another direction: P'yŏngyang, it was rumored, was about to fall to the control of the North Korean communists.

The retreating United Nations and South Korean forces were accompanied by a swarm of escaping North Koreans. People poured into the streets of P'yŏngyang to cross the Taedong River Bridge to flee to the south. On Sunday, December 3, 1950, Tong-hi's wife Sun-im and their eleven-year-old daughter, Hyŏn-ja, left for Sun-im's natal home, which was located across the Taedong River, leaving Tong-hi and their ten-year-old son, Hyŏn-kyu, at home. Tong-hi and his wife believed that women and female children should be evacuated before the Chinese troops invaded because of persistent rumors that the Chinese soldiers would rape young Korean women. After his wife and daughter left, Tong-hi went to church with his son to attend the regular Sunday service. Upon their return, they found that some South Korean army officers had brought a minibus to their home to take Tong-hi and his family to the south, knowing that the CPV invasion of P'yŏngyang was imminent.

When Tong-hi asked his parents to go with him, they refused. Besides Hyŏn-kyu, three other young men wished to escape in the minibus: Tong-hi's brother-in-law (his sister's husband), his cousin (his mother's sister's son), and a good friend. The minibus, already full of army officers, had few seats left. Tong-hi's parents kept insisting that the young should be evacuated over the old. Tong-hi and his parents could not argue long; the winter weather was cold and time was short, for the citizens of P'yŏngyang who wished to flee south were already filling the main street leading to the Taedong River Bridge, which could be blown up at any time. Tong-hi finally boarded the minibus with Hyŏn-kyu; every effort was made to save the male heir of the family. (With Hyŏn-su away from home for his military duty, Hyŏn-kyu was the next heir.)

As the minibus passed through crowded Chong-ro street, Hyŏn-kyu saw his mother and his sister walking with other refugees on their way to the bridge to the south. But the minibus could not stop; the fleeing crowds would have mobbed and completely stalled it. Tong-hi still remorses that he did not ask Maj. Kwang Ahn, who was in charge, to stop for his wife and young daughter, regardless of the reaction of the crowd. But he trusted that they would make it safely to Sun-im's home and never once thought that their separation would be more than temporary.

After crossing the bridge, Tong-hi and son walked for five days to Kaesŏng, rode a train from Kaesŏng to Seoul, and from there went by freight train to Pusan, a four-day trip that now takes four hours by express train. On December 18, 1950, fifteen days after they had left P'yŏngyang, Tong-hi and his young son arrived in the harbor city of Pusan. They did not have any shelter, nor did they have any money. Tong-hi soon found a job in the Third Army Hospital with the South Korean army, and Hyŏn-kyu worked in the hospital pharmacy as an office boy for meals and a place to sleep. Three days after Tong-hi started working, he was arrested by a South Korean intelligence officer and put in jail for a week, from December 24 to 31, 1950; he was suspected of being a North Korean spy. Through the efforts of his church minister and an American missionary, he was released. Tong-hi also learned from other refugees from P'yŏngyang that his wife and young daughter had given up trying to walk southward and had returned to P'yŏngyang because they were being outdistanced by the swiftly advancing Chinese troops.

In June 1951, thanks to the assistance of several church leaders, he was given the opportunity to help the many poverty-stricken victims of the war. Promised a supply of medicine for fifty patients per day by the United Nations relief organization, he began a free clinic for the poor in a tent on an empty lot, where he treated up to sixty people a day. Later, another refugee physician, a friend from Seoul, joined him to ease the workload, but the free clinic still remained short of physicians. At one time, more than two hundred patients a day were needing treatment, too many for the eleven-member team, which included but two physicians, to handle. The forty-four family members of the clinic's staff were sustained by the five hundred dollars per month in charity funds donated by American church organizations. Despite the heavy workload at the clinic in Pusan, the two physicians also visited doctorless villages once a month, administering to patients suffering from all kinds of disease. Tong-hi was truly utilizing his medical knowledge for the poor, as he had committed himself to do in his youth as a Christian. Because of the dedication of Tong-hi and his associates, the free clinic evolved into a modern hospital, which still serves the poor in Pusan, charging minimum fees. Tong-hi is still working in that hospital, which is where I conducted my interviews with him.

Considering the average life span of Koreans, Tong-hi's parents have probably passed away. Tong-hi is firmly convinced that his wife, Sun-im, his son, Hyŏn-su, who was drafted by the North Korean army, and his daughter, Hyŏn-ja, who was with her mother on the day of their separation, are alive in the north. "I often dream about my wife," he said. "Sometimes, I see her angry face. But whenever I see her in a dream, even if she snarls at me, it makes me happy all day long." He may not be overtly expressive about his longing for his wife, but he seems to think of her all the time. "She was not unusually pretty or anything like that. But, in many respects, she was a good-looking woman. Certainly, she was not any worse than I. Regardless of her looks, while I was living with her, I became attracted by her inner charm and wonderful personality and her total devotion to me and my parents. Not many women would have sacrificed themselves for their husbands as my wife did for me." Sun-im had been a good wife, a wise mother, and a filial daughter-in-law. The longer Tong-hi lived with his wife, he discovered, the more he loved her.

In Tong-hi's memory Sun-im was, above all else, a good daughter-in-law to his parents. Even when his jealous mother, who was competing with her daughter-in-law to love and be loved by her son, nagged her unreasonably, Sun-im tolerated her mother-in-law's tantrums, knowing they would not last more than one day at a time. Even though Sun-im's natal home was nearby, she seldom visited her parents, perhaps once or twice a year at the most, believing that her home was with her husband and his parents. Whenever they needed extra money, she was the one who had acquired it, either borrowing from someone or finding a part-time job to earn the extra money.

Tong-hi remembered the day he first felt the existence of a genuine love between himself and Sun-im: "One day while I was writing something inside my room, all of a sudden I felt that I was in love with her. I could not explain the feeling I had, but it was beyond the simple love that commonly occurs between ordinary husband and wife. I knew that I loved her dearly and that she loved me also. No one in the world could love me more than she did." He has never forgotten a song entitled "Sunset," which he learned from his wife, even though he seldom sings it. "I guess she taught me that song for me to sing in the sunset of my life like now," he said. Others have observed that when he sings the song "Going Home" at a church gathering, as he often does, they see tears in his eyes. He rarely mentions his family members in the north or shows his emotions to others. But he is always thinking about the painful separation from his family.

Those who cannot understand his love for his wife and his strong commitment to be faithful to her have often tried to persuade him to remarry. A few single women who have worked with him in the hospital and other charity organizations respected him greatly, liked him very much, and even fell in love with him. On one occasion he received a letter of proposal from a female physician who had emigrated to the United States. But for him remarriage is unthinkable. He cannot forget the love he has for his wife and firmly believes that such love goes far beyond just living with someone.

The ten-year-old son he took with him in the winter of 1950 has become a mature scholar of medicine and a professor at a respectable medical

school in Seoul. Although Tong-hi could go live with his son as many
elderly Koreans do, he refuses that comfortable life. Despite his age, he
still works at the hospital he founded, treating twenty or thirty patients a
day. He lives in a room at the hospital.

Tong-hi had been particularly moved by scenes from the reunion telethon broadcast on television in the summer of 1983. He confessed that he
could not control his longing for his family members who he believes are
still alive in the north. "Since in reality I cannot do anything about my
situation, I try to meet with my separated family members spiritually," he
said. He hopes that someday he will be able to see them again. He has a
firm conviction that dialogue between the north and south will eventually
lead to a resolution of their conflict. He talks about the pain of dispersal as
if he were talking about the pain of others, but he is really speaking of his
own pain.

CHAPTER 6

A Man Longs
for His Parents

Yong-mun Park was separated from his parents and taken south by his
sister-in-law in 1948 when he was fourteen years old. I have known him
since my freshman year in college, when we worked together on the student council. Although he was three years senior to me, we became close
friends and remained close until I went to America.

When I began planning this project, I consulted with Yong-mun first.
He assured me of his support and assistance and informed me that he was
already involved in background work for the North-South Red Cross talks
on family reunion. In addition to learning more about Yong-mun's own
history, I also wanted to know about the overall north-south discussion
and its prospects.

I could not even list how often I interviewed him or when those interviews took place. Sometimes, they were inside his car while we were driv-
ing or in restaurants over dinner, and at other times they were at a *taepo-
jib*, or a stand-up bar. I spent hours at his office working on my project.
His experiences working with North Koreans in various capacities were
interesting. Except for a few high-echelon officials in the South Korean
Central Intelligence Agency, he probably knew more about the outcome
of the North-South Red Cross dialogue than anyone else. He was my most
helpful and trustworthy informant, and our relationship was informal and
relaxed.

Yong-mun Park was born in T'ogo-ri, Myŏngch'ŏn, Hamkyŏng Puk-do province in North Korea in 1934. Although by the 1980s he had lived in Seoul longer than he had lived in T'ogo-ri, his affection for his hometown was still strong. He fondly remembered his childhood there, when he lived with his parents, siblings, and friends. When he spoke of the scenery around his hometown—including the two beautiful mountains Chaedŏk and Ch'ilbo and the Sea of Japan across the hills—he became very nostalgic. He longed to go back, to renew his memories. But the political barriers between the north and south make his return to T'ogo-ri impossible.

Whenever he sees or hears about *myŏng-t'ae,* or dried pollack, he is reminded of his hometown. The name *myŏng-t'ae* is derived from the name of his county, Myŏngch'ŏn. According to a Korean fable, a fisherman caught an unusual fish, one he did not recognize. He inquired about the unknown fish, but no one seemed to be able to identify it. The county commissioner of Myŏngch'ŏn called it *myŏng-t'ae,* combining the name of the county, *myŏng,* and the surname of the fisherman who caught the fish, *T'ae.*[1] *Myŏng-t'ae* is one of the most popular fishes among Koreans. It is available along most of the eastern seacoast of the northern peninsula, but the varieties from Myŏngch'ŏn and its vicinity, particularly the well-dried golden fish from Myŏngch'ŏn, are considered the best. South Koreans also call it *puk'ŏ,* meaning "fish from the north." It is considered indispensable for the table prepared during ancestor worship rites. Yong-mun's affection for his hometown is commingled with the strong affection that Koreans have for this fish.

Yong-mun graduated from a respected law school in Seoul. He then went to graduate school in law, specializing in humanitarian law, and received his master's and doctoral degrees. He is the author of several books and many articles on human rights. He taught international law in a university in Seoul. Among many other activities, he devotes much time to the management of his kin group organization, the Myŏngch'ŏn Park lineage, a branch of a large kin group.

According to the lineage's genealogical records, the Parks originated from a common ancestor in Ch'ungju in Ch'ungch'ŏng Puk-do province in South Korea. The known ancestor of the Parks in Myŏngch'ŏn and other places in Hamkyŏng Puk-do province was Sŏ Park, who relocated to Myŏngch'ŏn from Ch'ungju toward the end of the Koryŏ dynasty (918–1392) or the beginning of the Yi dynasty (1392–1910). The genealogical records do not specify why Sŏ Park moved from Ch'ungch'ŏng Puk-do to a northern province of Hamkyŏng Puk-do, but since Sŏ Park had once held a district governorship of Ch'ungju, he could have been sent north as a political exile. Sŏ Park started a family in Myŏngch'ŏn and created his own lineage, the Myŏngch'ŏn branch of the Ch'ungju Park clan. When the lineage updated its genealogical records in 1937, it found that twenty-two successive generations of Myŏngch'ŏn Parks had lived in the Myŏngch'ŏn area. In 1945, in the vicinity of Myŏngch'ŏn, it counted three major lineages with thirty minor lineages. Other lineages are scattered throughout other counties in Hamkyŏng Puk-do and Hamkyŏng Nam-do and have also been located in Chientao, Manchuria, and the Maritime Province of Russia. Most of the ancestral graves, including that of Sŏ Park, the founder of the Myŏngch'ŏn Park lineage, are in Myŏng-ch'ŏn, near Yong-mun's village of T'ogo-ri.

Yong-mun's father, Han-kyu Park, was born and reared in T'ogo-ri. His family had lived in the same house for many generations. Han-kyu was a Confucian scholar and became a respected elder in his lineage as the *chongson,* or the eldest son of the heir of the lineage. In his position as *chongson,* he considered ancestor worship rites as being of utmost importance and dedicated himself to their faithful observance. He observed ancestor worship services for five generations of his ancestors. Roger L. Janelli and Dawnhee Yim Janelli have indicated that the eldest son, who is responsible for the ancestral rites, keeps four generations of the wooden tablets of his ancestors. But some orthodox Confucianists keep five generations of ancestral tablets and observe their worship rites.[2] Han-kyu's family shrine was filled with wooden tablets symbolizing the spirits of dead ancestors.[3] (Paper tablets and sometimes photographs of the dead ones are now used in place of the traditional wooden tablets.)

As the *chongson* of the lineage, Han-kyu was one of the most respected persons in T'ogo-ri. Moreover, he was a landlord with extensive landholdings. But his privileges, reputation, and position in the village were altered when the communists gained control over North Korea upon the liberation of Korea from Japan in 1945. In 1946 he and his family were ostracized from the village by the communists on the grounds that the family owned too much land and had exploited the tenant farmers too long. The family was relocated to the port city of Sŏngjin, at the southeastern tip of Hamkyŏng Puk-do and lost almost everything they had. Yong-mun remembers that when the family was packing, his father loaded the wooden ancestral tablets in the oxcart before any other belongings, as if he were taking all of his ancestors. They could have taken more household belongings had his father not brought the tablets with him. In Sŏngjin the family had only a marginal living.

Yong-mun's older brother, Yong-ki, a small businessman, visited P'yŏngyang often to buy things to sell in Sŏngjin. On these trips he became acquainted with a guide who knew the underground route to the south. The guide told Yong-ki that for a small fee he would lead his family across the thirty-eighth parallel. Yong-ki decided to flee south, taking the illegal route. He knew that as long as he lived in the north he would be discriminated against because of his background.[4] Yong-ki begged his parents to go with him, but they refused to do so.

Han-kyu refused for several reasons. It would be too risky for the entire family to try to escape together across the well-guarded thirty-eighth parallel. And as the *chongson*, Han-kyu believed that he should remain as close as possible to the graves of his ancestors. Further, he could not carry all of his dead ancestors' tablets with him if he did decide to cross the border. But most important, the three years of mourning that were traditionally observed for deceased parents among Confucian families had not yet elapsed since the death of Han-kyu's father, and like most orthodox Confucianists he believed that an even longer period of mourning demonstrated greater filial piety. Han-kyu also wished to observe the traditional mourning for his deceased father as near as possible to his father's grave. Fleeing to the south would not enable him to do so. (In earlier times the chief mourner was not supposed to meet strangers, to travel, to dress in luxurious or colorful clothes, to trim his hair, or even to bathe.) Although Han-kyu decided to remain in the north, he wished to secure the continuation of his family line in a safe place. He thought the south would be more secure than any place in the north, including Sŏngjin. So he approved the plan of his eldest son, Yong-ki, to flee south. In 1947 Yong-ki and his wife departed Sŏngjin, leaving behind the rest of the family.

In the south Yong-ki demonstrated his business talent. He ran a soap manufacturing factory, which although not large, supported his family. In 1948, a year after their flight, Yong-ki's wife Hi-ryŏng infiltrated back into Sŏngjin to bring the rest of her husband's family to the south. Her father-in-law was still adamant about staying in Sŏngjin, hoping to return to T'ogo-ri someday. Yong-mun remembered the day his sister-in-law returned to Sŏngjin: "I could not believe her courage and strength. She had come all the way from Seoul to Sŏngjin, braving the danger along the guarded border of the thirty-eighth parallel. She even carried her baby on her back during that trip." Although Hi-ryŏng failed to persuade her parents-in-law to flee south, at her father-in-law's request she took Yong-mun and his younger sister with her.

Yong-mun's journey from Sŏngjin to Seoul was difficult and dangerous, but in the company of his twenty-nine-year-old sister-in-law he was unaware of any danger. He simply followed her. At fourteen, Yong-mun had only a general idea of what was going on, and many years later he could not remember how his fleeing party had managed to cross the parallel. He vaguely recalled that they had taken mostly backroads and had crossed the border between midnight and early morning. However, "I vividly remember the moment of my arrival in Seoul," Yong-mun said. "As soon as I saw the Tongrip-mun, the Independence Gate built of stone, which is in Yŏngch'ŏn at the northwestern edge of the city, I knew that I was in Seoul."

Contact between Yong-mun's family in the north and in the south did not completely cease after Yong-mun settled in Seoul in 1948. His mother somehow managed to cross the thirty-eighth parallel and came to Seoul several times to see her family. She also brought with her some northern products that were rare in the south, including the dried *myŏng-t'ae*, and sold them. When she returned to the north, she took some southern products that were expensive or unobtainable in the north, including such items as medicines and electric appliances. She made several such trips back and forth.

Yong-mun particularly remembers a trip his mother made to Seoul in 1949. It had been very risky, as the border guard had been intensified. She had come especially to deliver Yong-mun's school records so that he could enroll in a school in Seoul.

The family insisted that she stay with them and not return to North Korea. There were many indications that her illegal crossings and smuggling would become impossible. Many small-scale border skirmishes were already occurring along the thirty-eighth parallel. John Merrill reported that "border incidents also increased markedly as the August 15 date for the transfer of authority to the Rhee government approached, and American troops began to turn over their positions on the parallel to their South Korean counterparts; the last U.S. tactical forces, however, did not leave until June 1949."[5] Many people warned that with the withdrawal of the United States occupation forces there might be an all-out war between the north and south. Although Yong-mun and his brother and sister begged their mother earnestly not to return, she was passionately determined to do so. She was as stubborn as her husband had been.

Yong-mun's mother's resolute refusal to stay with her children in Seoul had nothing to do with ideology, for she cared nothing for ideology. She would have been happy anywhere, as long as her family members could live together harmoniously and comfortably. Her determination to go home was partially based on her Confucian virtue as a wife to follow her husband in marriage. Besides, she loved her husband dearly, even though, in accordance with Korean custom, she could not overtly express her love. But Yong-mun's mother had another reason for returning to North Korea; she had to look after one of her granddaughters, Myŏng-ok, the daughter of her eldest daughter. She had a special affection for Myŏng-ok because her parents had died young, and she had had no one else to take care of her.

Myŏng-ok's mother, Yong-suk, was the eldest daughter and the eldest of seven sons and daughters. She had married T'ae-ha Son from another village in the same county. T'ae-ha was an unusually progressive person for his time and a strong anti-Japanese nationalist. While T'ae-ha was going to university in Japan, he became actively involved in anti-Japanese movements. He also organized a movement in his home county during vacations there. He became a target of the Japanese colonial police; whenever he came home, a plainclothes Japanese policeman followed him. About the time he completed his schooling in Japan, T'ae-ha became involved in socialist activities and became a communist sympathizer. Like many Korean communists, he identified socialism or communism as an organized means for fighting Japanese colonial rule. Being leftist or communist became synonymous with being anti-Japanese.[6] Because of his communism, T'ae-ha was arrested by the Japanese police, and he died in jail before Korea was liberated from Japan. T'ae-ha's death was such a shock to his wife Yong-suk that she subsequently died, leaving little Myŏng-ok in the care of her grandmother. Yong-mun's mother reared Myŏng-ok as if she were her own daughter. In fact, she was nearly the same age as Yong-mun, her uncle.

The family had thought about bringing Myŏng-ok to Seoul to live with them there. But Myŏng-ok had become involved in the communist movement, knowing that her father had died for its cause and the anti-Japanese movement. She believed that she had a special duty to help the communist revolution. Further, she enjoyed a favored position, being the daughter of a communist who had sacrificed his life for the communist cause. She entered a special military school for young women and became involved in various party activities.

Yong-mun's mother thought that since Myǒng-ok did not have anybody else to look after her, particularly regarding her marriage, she should take care of her. Yong-mun speculated, "My mother might have stayed with us in Seoul if she hadn't been worrying about Myǒng-ok. Instead of going back to the north, she could have tried to bring my father back to the south to live with us. But again I'm second-guessing." Yong-mun thought that his mother had been very happy to see that her sons were doing well and that she did not have to worry about them. The heir of her family line was well secured in a safe place in the south.

The visit of Yong-mun's mother in 1949 was her last. Shortly thereafter, in 1950, the war broke out, and the two sides of the family were no longer able to maintain contact with each other.

When the Korean War began, Yong-mun was too young to be drafted or mobilized either by the South Korean army or by the northern forces that later occupied Seoul. The family's sedate life in Seoul was destroyed, however, and they once more became refugees. Luckily, they managed to escape to Pusan before the communists invaded Seoul.

Yong-mun's older brother, Yong-ki, was drafted by the South Korean army. His military status eventually allowed him to visit his hometown in the north and see his parents in Sǒngjin. One day in late October 1950 Yong-ki stopped by T'ogo-ri and was astounded to find his parents back in their home. They had just moved back from Sǒngjin to T'ogo-ri during the communists' retreat farther northward. It was a thrilling reunion for Yong-ki and his parents. They firmly believed that their country would soon be reunited and that their family members could once again live together. In Yong-ki's eyes the village had not changed at all since his family had been banished from it four years before. But the interior of the family's house had been remodeled by the communists, who had used it as a public hall for village meetings. Yong-ki's parents were eager and excited as they busily prepared to resettle in their old house.

They had no way of knowing what would transpire during the coming winter. Without warning, the Chinese crossed the Korean-Manchurian border and changed the course of the war. As time went on, more Chinese forces were engaged on the battle front, and by December 1950 the United Nations and South Korean forces started to retreat, withdrawing from the parts of North Korea they had occupied. Yong-ki knew that his parents should be evacuated to Seoul, even if the withdrawal was only tactical and temporary, but he could not leave his squad in the midst of the retreat to arrange for the safety of his parents.

As he departed with his unit, Yong-ki saw many North Korean refugees desperate to board any kind of moving vehicle. He felt toward them as he would have felt toward his own family, but he could do nothing to help them. When he arrived in Hŭngnam harbor, Yong-ki hoped that his parents would be there among the hundreds of thousands of other refugees. Unfortunately, they were not, but even if they had been, he probably would not have been able to locate them. His reunion with his parents in their T'ogo-ri home in late October was their last meeting.

Yong-mun and Yong-ki believed that their parents did not try to go to South Korea. During the reunion telethon in the summer of 1983, I asked Yong-mun if it were possible that his parents had come to the south somehow during the winter retreat but simply had not been able to locate their family. Yong-mun was certain that this had not happened: "My mother knew where we lived in Seoul. She had been in Seoul several times before the war. If my parents had somehow managed to flee, they would not have had any problem finding where we lived. My brother did not even want to move to another place, because he worried that they might not be able to find us."

Yong-mun grew up, married, and became the father of two children. Despite many difficult years, during which he was twice uprooted from his home as a refugee, he became a successful man, personally and professionally.

Yong-mun's indomitable determination to be successful made him seek the finest education available. His benevolent personality led him to devote his career to aiding the underprivileged, although his modest and unpretentious personality prevented him from admitting that his work with refugees was not by chance. His educational background would have allowed him to choose an easier job with greater financial rewards, but he had chosen instead to work with various relief organizations.

Yong-mun played an important role during the North-South Red Cross conference regarding families dispersed during the war. He was particularly interested in the north-south talks because of the dispersal of his own family, especially the separation from his parents. He firmly believes that the reunion of separated family members is not "a desire of the family" but "a right of the family" as stated at the Geneva conference on humanitarian law held in the spring of 1976.

Although Yong-mun was separated from his father at a fairly early age, he seems to have been influenced greatly by him. Yong-mun's appreciation of Confucian ethics and classics, his literary knowledge of Chinese characters, and his artistic ability in Chinese calligraphy were exceptional for any Korean of his age and can be attributed to Han-yuk's tutelage. Finding someone with Yong-mun's abilities would be unlikely today, especially among young Koreans who have had extensive Western educations, though there are similarly skilled Koreans among older generations in rural villages.

Yong-mun became particularly interested in his lineage. By studying the genealogical records of his clan, he was even able to trace the original ancestors of his clan in the south who had migrated to the north. His curiosity about his family roots may stem from his efforts as a refugee and someone who was separated from his parents in adolescence to find his identity. However, he believes that discovering one's past through kinship ties and genealogical records does much more than establish one's personal identity. For Korean refugees, given their particular social pattern and structure, the genealogical movement has had many practical implications. The genealogies have been instrumental in locating missing family members by the use of kin networks, which have strengthened relationships and fellowship among the members and have developed organizations for mutual assistance and support. Currently, Yong-mun holds a key position in the Myŏngch'ŏn branch of his lineage, which was first organized in the south by members who had fled just before the Korean War.

The first organizational meeting of the South Korean branch of the Myŏngch'ŏn Parks kin group was held at Ch'angkyŏng-wŏn, an old palace of the Yi dynasty, on April 17, 1949, a year before the outbreak of war. A zealous member of the Myŏngch'ŏn Parks lineage had carried the six-volume 1937 edition of their genealogical records with him when he went south. Instead of taking other belongings, he had chosen to bring the heavy records—illustrating the value Koreans can attach to their genealogy. The number of the participants at the organizational meeting was small, but it was a good beginning. The members were drawn even more closely together in exile than they had been in their home of Myŏngch'ŏn.

Regular meetings of the lineage members in Seoul were interrupted by the Korean War. Most of those who lived in Seoul became refugees again, fleeing further south as the northern forces advanced. After the war ended, the members resumed their meetings in Seoul on the fifth of May each year. Their membership had increased greatly by the addition of those who had fled during the war: the total number of families had grown from sixty to over one hundred. As the number of members increased, the organization became more formal. It also needed funds to operate; however, no one could afford to donate the required sum. Most of the refugees were struggling to survive and could not support the organization. Until the 1970s the lineage limited its activities to maintaining close ties and promoting fellowship among its members.

The most urgent business of the organization was to update the old edition of their genealogy and to compile a separate one for those who had come to South Korea, tracing each member in accordance with the original records. Because most members were from Myŏngch'ŏn and its vicinity, they knew each other from before the war. But it would be necessary to identify the members who were from Manchuria and other provinces of North Korea. Without identification of all the relationships, particularly in order of generation, members might address each other incorrectly. In accordance with the Korean kinship rule, members were not called by their personal names but by specific kinship terms. These terms indicate age, generation, and the kin distance from one relative to another.[7] In addition, teknonymous and geononymous terms were used. A junior member with a child (or children) would probably be addressed teknonymously, and often also geononymously, by a senior member. Teknonymy refers to the practice of calling an adult not by his or her own name but by the name of a child, adding the relationship between the child and the adult: "So-and-so's father" is an example. Geononymy refers to "the name of a person's place of origin or current residence [that] is added to the appropriate kinship term to distinguish a particular relative (or relative who has been given a fictive kinship term) from others to whom the same kinship term is applied."[8]

In the late 1960s the members of the South Korean branch of the Myŏngch'ŏn Parks lineage created a formal organization, called the Association of the Myŏngch'ŏn Parks Lineage in the South. This association includes an elder as the symbolic head of the association and has a president and a vice-president elected by the participating members to represent the association. Each family unit has one vote. Beneath the president and vice-president is the executive director, who actually runs the organization, assisted by three directors: director for general business affairs, director for publications, and director for scholarships. In addition, the executive director is responsible for supervising the Myŏngch'ŏn Club, which consists of middle-aged male members who do the essential work of the large association.

The main difference between the Association of the Myŏngch'ŏn Parks Lineage in the South and the Myŏngch'ŏn Club is that the latter is an ad hoc group under the control of the former. The club is distinguished from the larger clan by its composition. The association includes all the members whose names are listed in the genealogy: all males, their spouses, and their unmarried daughters are regular members, and the married daughters of members are classified as associate members. The Myŏngch'ŏn Club is exclusively for middle-aged men, discriminating not only on the basis of gender but also on the basis of age.

The main body of the organization also discriminates against women. When the daughters of members marry, they are automatically reclassified as associate members. They are not allowed to vote in the election for the president and vice-president of the association, and their spouses and children are ineligible for membership. Although the association adopted some democratic forms, including the presidential and vice-presidential election, it retains the traditional agnatic organization of the Korean kinship system, with its emphasis on patrilineal descent.

In 1975 Yong-mun was appointed the executive director of the Association of the Myŏngch'ŏn Parks Lineage in the South and became responsible for running the association and administering the Myŏngch'ŏn Club under the direction of the president and vice-president. His primary duties were to promote and maintain fellowship and close ties among the members; to raise funds for scholarships and award them to needy members; and to prepare and publish the genealogy, the essential document that would allow the members to trace their family relationships, calculate the distance between members, and address one another properly. In 1971, thanks to the donation of the then oldest member of the lineage (he occupied the position of the elder, whose ranking in the association is the most prestigious and who is a symbolic representative of the association), Yong-mun was able to make copies of the six-volume genealogy brought south before the Korean War.

As the members became more prosperous, the funding of the association improved. In 1975 Yong-mun initiated a project to compile information for the publication of a supplementary genealogy devoted to those Parks who were living in the south. The final version of the supplementary edition was published in 1978; it covered one hundred families in South Korea, plus ten families in Japan, the United States, and Canada. This modern edition had a few special characteristics that traditional Korean genealogical records did not have. The book took the same format as the others, listing the names of the members in genealogical order from the common ancestors, with dates of birth and the dates of death if deceased.

But almost all traditional Korean genealogical records were written in Chinese characters only; Yong-mun's project included a Korean translation of the Chinese characters, making the book easier to read for those not familiar with Chinese.

The other new feature was the listing of the names of females, including the spouses of the male members and both the unmarried and married daughters of the members. Historically, Korean females were not supposed to have had personal names, and even when they did have them, they were never included in genealogies of either their own lineages or their husbands' lineages. Females' names were thus free from the generation names, whereas males' names had to follow the name of the generation. In the genealogy of my own lineage, as an example of a traditional record, the name of my father-in-law, and not the name of my wife, is written in a space provided next to my name, and then his daughter along with his origin of lineage is specified. Also, beside my name in the same generation line, instead of the names of my three married sisters are the names of their husbands and their lineages. In dropping this system, the supplementary genealogy published by the Myŏngch'ŏn Parks lineage was quite innovative, and it has helped upgrade the status of its female members.[9]

Another notable innovation in the supplementary edition of the Parks genealogy was the addition of the *t'aekho,* or the name of a family or household. The *t'aekho* differs from a surname and is a label attached to each family within a given lineage.[10] The *t'aekho* is determined by the occupation or position of a direct ancestor of the family, such as a high government office. The *t'aekho* is a source of pride in this case and would be inherited through the generations by the eldest son, following the rule of primogeniture. If *yangban* families do not have an ancestor in a high government position through a direct ancestral line, the *t'aekho* is replaced by the name of the place where the wife of the eldest male, usually the head of the household, resided before her marriage.[11] This is comparable to geononymy.[12] The *t'aekho* is extremely useful in identifying one's affiliation to a particular lineage. It was most useful and appropriate to include it in the genealogy of those persons who were separated from their family members during the Korean War. Yong-mun's zeal and his concern for helping his kinsmen in finding their missing family members are reflected in the publication of the genealogy.

Another important function of the association under the direction of Yong-mun was to raise funds for and award scholarships to the children of the members. Yong-mun and the other lineage members strongly believed that education was the avenue to success regardless of the careers the young people might choose. Yong-mun himself had needed such aid when he was obtaining his education. This scholarship system is an outgrowth of the traditional Korean kinship system, particularly of its solidarity and its management of the common property of a clan. Many Korean clans own property in common to support the scholarly pursuits of their members, as well as to provide funds for their ancestor worship rites and to maintain the shrines for their ancestors.[13]

Yong-mun has devoted much of his time and effort to developing close relationships among the members. The association has been particularly active in assisting members to become financially independent. The association also donates funds for weddings and funerals. Because most members do not have immediate kin, they help one another, and for many members the organization has been like a big family. Members have filled the empty spaces in one another's lives caused by the separation of their families. Yong-mun's dedication to the association was one of the best ways he could demonstrate filial piety to his parents.

When the South Korean Red Cross was preparing the application forms for those who wished to register for the reunion telethon, Yong-mun insisted that a column for kin-group affiliation be included. In addition to the other background information about an individual, this would be important in identifying lost family members, as there are so many identical surnames in Korea. His suggestion resulted from his experiences in working with his clan organization.

Yong-mun has done more than his share for his clan members and for other North Korean refugees. But "regardless of what I have done for others," Yong-mun said regretfully, "I'm still not doing what I should do for my parents as a son, that is, observing the rites of ancestor worship for them." Yong-mun assumes that both of his parents are dead, but he cannot perform the regular ancestor worship rites because he does not know the dates of their deaths, if indeed they are deceased. (Regular ancestor worship rites are offered on the death dates of the ancestors as well as on holidays.) Yong-mun's longing for his parents has become deeper and more profound as he has grown older. I knew I could not ask him, "Don't you wish you could show your lovely family, your two children and beautiful wife, to your parents?" Instead of asking and answering such a question, Yong-mun and I drank *soju,* Korean vodka. He knew my question, and I knew his answer.

CHAPTER 7

The Reunion Movement
and the Reunion Telethon

The dispersal of Korean families resulting from World War II and the fratricidal Korean War was the most devastating aftermath of the two wars.
Until recently, the governments of both North and South Korea have done
little except to issue occasional humanitarian slogans, and there has been
little progress in assisting sundered families to reunite with their relatives,
some of whom have now been separated from them for over forty years.

THE REUNION MOVEMENT

The issue of allowing South Koreans who were kidnapped by North
Korea to return to their families was first addressed during the negotiations that lasted from July 10, 1951, to July 27, 1953. Through the United
Nations command, the South Korean government demanded the inclu-
sion of a clause calling for the repatriation of persons kidnapped by the
north during the war, and the United Nations command was able to obtain
a provision for the repatriation of displaced persons in the armistice agreement between the north and south. This provision emphasized the principle of voluntary repatriation.[1] The Truman administration vehemently
insisted that it be applied to the exchange of prisoners of war. Details of

repatriation were left to the Committee for the Return of Displaced Civilians (CRDC), which consisted of four field-grade officers (lieutenants), two from each side. The CRDC was formed and held its first conference at P'anmunjŏm on December 11, 1953. Both sides agreed on nine points, including when and where an exchange should take place.

From January 5 to February 17, 1954, the South Korean government received applications from displaced persons who wished to return to the north. The number of applicants was seventy-six. On February 18 the committee members of the United Nations command turned over the list to the communists.[2] In the meantime, the communists had provided their list of nineteen civilians who desired repatriation to the south. All these civilians turned out to be of foreign nationalities; there were eleven Turks and eight Russians. Of the seventy-six persons who desired repatriation to the north, thirty-seven changed their minds at the last moment, and two were proven to be North Korean espionage agents. On March 1 the United Nations command released the remaining thirty-seven applicants to North Korea, and the communist side handed over the nineteen foreigners.[3]

The outcome of the March 1 repatriation effort clearly indicated the weakness of the CRDC; it had been assigned a task too big and too politically sensitive for its four lower-echelon field officers to tackle. The naïveté of the committee was shown in its schedule for the repatriation, which had allowed less than two months to announce the exchange, publicize it, and receive and screen the applications. The arrangements had been inadequate.

Seeing the committee's lack of success, the South Korean government sought a solution elsewhere. Foreign Minister Yŏng-t'ae Pyŏn took the case to the International Committee of the Red Cross (ICRC) at its Asian conference in Geneva in the summer of 1954.[4] On January 31, 1955, the ICRC sent official letters to both North and South Korea to determine whether or not they were willing to accept its direct intervention regarding repatriation. The South Korean government expressed its willingness, but there was no response from the P'yŏngyang regime. The ICRC recognized its limitations in monitoring the problem.[5]

The ICRC had been persistent in trying to assist family members who had been dispersed during the war, regardless of the adherence of the two Korean regimes to the Geneva convention.[6] At its eighteenth conference in Toronto, Canada, in 1952, while the war was going on, the ICRC had adopted a resolution to help the large number of persons who were sepa-

rated from their homes and from their families. The South Korean government had dispatched a delegate to the Toronto conference to ask the
ICRC to aid in accounting for 17,500 kidnapped persons and 2,200 others
to be repatriated to the south. The ICRC had received no response from
North Korea.[7] (The resolution has been repeatedly reaffirmed in subsequent international conferences, and all governments and national societies of the Red Cross have been urged to intensify their efforts to facilitate
the reunion of dispersed persons.)[8]

From June 15 to August 5, 1956, the South Korean Red Cross launched
a unilateral nationwide registration drive to gather more detailed information on people who had been kidnapped by North Korea during the
Korean War. The Red Cross reported that this registration brought 7,034
additional entries to the previous list. The names of the additional registrants were sent to the ICRC by the South Korean Red Cross in October.[9]
At the nineteenth conference of the ICRC in New Delhi, India, in November 1957, the ICRC presented to North Korea a list of 337 living persons
from the South Korean registrants. At the same time, the North Korean
Red Cross demanded an account of 14,132 refugees from the north. The
South Korean Red Cross responded to the northern inquiry that "14,112
out of 14,132 refugees had not been kidnapped but defected to the south of
their own accord."[10]

From 1957 to the early 1970s the two Red Cross societies in Korea maintained a low profile. The rhetoric of the 1950s was ended when it became
apparent that political circumstances prevented any solution to the problem of sundered families; a more realistic effort was launched to locate
dispersed family members within each country. The political milieu in the
south during the 1960s, however, with the student revolution against the
Syngman Rhee regime in April 1960 and the military coup of May 1961,
diverted attention from efforts to reunite separated families. A daily newspaper, the *Hankook Ilbo*, took up the initiative and tried to locate separated
family members within the south and reunite them. From January 1, 1961,
to December 1967, the newspaper reported on sixty-three orphans who
were in an orphanage near Seoul and included individual photographs,
names, ages, sex, a brief sketch of their separation, and names of their parents if available. But this approach was not successful. I was unable to find
out how many other orphans had been reported on in the newspapers
during those years. Nor was I able to find out how many orphans had
been reunited with their families. When I visited the research section of
the *Hankook Ilbo* during my fieldwork in the summer of 1983, ironically one

of their files that contained the information I was looking for was missing. No other sources had reported on these figures.

A second *Hankook Ilbo* campaign lasted from 1974 to 1976. This campaign also failed to generate the enthusiastic support of the potential seekers or the public that the *Hankook Ilbo* had anticipated. The newspaper published 3,510 names in one hundred installments, but only 170 reunions were accomplished. This campaign was, however, the first of its kind by a nongovernmental organization, other than the Red Cross, to be initiated on a nationwide scale.

Among the nongovernmental organizations that devoted their efforts to the reunion of separated family members in the 1960s were the provisional offices of five North Korean provinces in Seoul. Each provincial office had gatherings twice a year, in the spring and fall, designating different days for its prefectures. Sometimes families were reunited at these gatherings. In 1963 each provincial association began publishing its own monthly newsletter, which included a special column for locating missing family members. The five provincial associations together also started a monthly magazine called *Ibuk Kong Bo* (North Korean News), which also had such a column. No accurate statistics on the number of people reunited through these monthly newsletters and magazines are available.

Participation in the Olympic Games allowed a couple of Korean athletes to either meet or communicate with their separated family members. On October 9, 1964, a North Korean woman sprinter, Kŭm-dan Sin, whose father, Mun-jun Sin, had fled south during the war, was able to see her father during the 1964 Summer Olympics in Tokyo. On February 17, 1971, a North Korean skater, P'il-hwa Han, who was attending the pre-Olympic Games in Sapporo, Japan, to prepare for the 1972 Winter Olympics, had a chance to telephone her brother, P'il-sŏng, in South Korea, by arrangement of the *Asahi Shimbun*, a Japanese daily newspaper. The brother and sister, who had been separated twenty-one years, talked for thirty minutes.[11]

Twice in 1963, on January 21 in Lausanne and on May 15 in Hong Kong, representatives of the Olympic committees of North and South Korea had met and discussed the possible formation of a single team for the forthcoming games in Japan. But the negotiations broke down and were ended by July 26, 1963. In April 1979 the north proposed a unified team for the thirty-fifth World Table Tennis Championship Game to be held in P'yŏng-yang. Negotiations were again unsuccessful. As a result, South Korea's team was not allowed to participate. In May 1984 there were three rounds of inter-Korean sports talks on forming a joint team for the 1984 Los Angeles Olympics, but an agreement could not be reached. On August 17, 1984, the president of the South Korean Olympic Committee and Korean Amateur Sports Association proposed to reopen the sports talks, but on August 27 the North Korean counterpart rejected the south's proposal. Several contacts have been made between the Olympic committees of the north and south about a joint team for the 1988 Olympics scheduled in Seoul, but these, too, have been unsuccessful.

The 1960s were years of considerable hostility and tension between North and South Korea, culminating in the seizure of the American intelligence-gathering ship *Pueblo* by North Korean forces on January 23, 1968. The 1970s offered more promising prospects for establishing good rapport between North and South Korea. The trend toward peaceful co-existence that emerged in the 1960s between the East and the West evolved into political detente in the 1970s. South Korean president Chung-hee Park declared a new policy of north-south relations in his National Inde-pendence Day address of August 15, 1970. Park asked North Korea "to stop . . . preparing for war" and to "participate in peaceful competition to de-termine which political system, free democracy or communism, can better serve the people's well-being—a competition in development, construc-tion, and creativeness." [12]

Park's declaration prompted the South Korean Red Cross to open di-rect talks on the reunion of dispersed families with its counterpart in the north without going through the ICRC or any other third party. On August 12, 1971, Tu-sŏn Choi, president of the South Korean Red Cross, made public a proposal to the North Korean Red Cross for discussions to bring about the prompt solution of purely humanitarian problems exist-ing between the north and south. The response from the North Korean Red Cross was swift and positive. On August 14, over P'yŏngyang radio, the North Korean Red Cross not only acknowledged the necessity of such talks but also proposed to expand their scope beyond the limits of the southern proposal. The North Korean Red Cross also wished to include other topics such as allowing free travel and mutual visits between families, relatives, and even friends separated in the north and south. [13]

Despite the difficult task ahead, public excitement ran high and hopes for an agreement between the north and south were tempered only by the fear that the talks would be used for political purposes. Even cautious ob-servers believed that the opening of the talks was itself a most important accomplishment. On August 15, 1971, South Korean president Park assured his government's support for the Red Cross talks in his National Independence Day address.

At noon on August 20 messengers of the Red Cross societies from both sides met at the Neutral Nations Supervisory Commission (NNSC) conference room in the P'anmunjŏm truce village in the DMZ and exchanged official documents on the family search campaign. The first contact between the messengers lasted for only three minutes, but it was historic nonetheless, for it opened a channel for dialogue between the two regimes. From August 20 to September 16, through five contacts by messenger at the same place, the two sides were able to reach an agreement on the date, place, number of delegates, and exchange of the lists of the delegates for preliminary talks. The dialogue had proceeded without any major obstacles, and a few minor differences had been easily resolved.

The two delegations selected for the preliminary talks, Yŏn-ju Kim and ten attendants from the south and T'ae-hŭi Kim and eight attendants from the north, met at the NNSC conference room in the P'anmunjŏm truce village on September 20. The purpose of the preliminary talks was to establish a format for the main talks later. This time, however, things were not to go so smoothly. Obstacles clearly remained between the two sides. The preliminary discussions, focusing only on procedure and a date for the main talks, were to take almost a year and involve twenty-five sessions and sixteen working-level meetings.

Through the third session each side made significant concessions. Two important agreements were reached: to establish permanent liaison offices at P'anmunjŏm and to install a direct telephone line between the liaison offices (at Freedom House on the south side of P'anmunjŏm for the South Korean Red Cross and at P'anmungak for the North Korean Red Cross). On September 22 the direct telephone line was installed: it was the first telephone link between the north and south since the partition of the country.

As the talks proceeded further, the negotiators found out that concessions and compromises were not as easily reached as in the earlier sessions. The North Korean delegation insisted that not only families and relatives but also "friends" should be included in the category of suffering people to be helped by the Red Cross campaign. The North Korean Red Cross also demanded that separated people be allowed to have "free travel" and "free visits" with each other, without any restrictions. The South Korean delegation thought the northern demand unrealistic, if not a political attempt to divert the Red Cross talks to discussion of unification. At this point discussions were deadlocked, and no significant progress was made toward reaching an agreement on agenda items for the main talks.

In October, in the midst of an unproductive closed-door session of the preliminary talks, the third-ranking South Korean delegate, Hong-jin Chŏng, handed a secret memorandum to his North Korean counterpart, Tŏk-hyŏn Kim, in which he proposed secret negotiations between the two. Kim was deputy chief of the northern delegation and was listed as the North Korean Red Cross information division chief, but he was actually a high-ranking officer of the Central Committee of the North Korean Worker's Party (KWP). Chŏng was listed as chief of the conference management division of the South Korean Red Cross, but he was also a ranking officer of the South Korean Central Intelligence Agency (KCIA). Kim readily accepted Chŏng's proposal. They met secretly, apart from the Red Cross preliminary talks. By request, Chŏng visited P'yŏngyang secretly from March 28 to 31, 1972, and in return, Kim visited Seoul from April 19 to 21. By April 29, as the result of their meetings, a direct telephone line between the offices of the KCIA and KWP was installed.[14]

The visits of Chŏng and Kim paved the way for a secret mission by the director of the KCIA, Hu-rak Lee, accompanied by Chŏng and a physician and a bodyguard, to P'yŏngyang from May 2 to 5 to meet North Korean president Il-sŏng Kim. Lee's trip to the north was kept secret in the south, but Lee had informed the chief of the American Central Intelligence Agency in South Korea of his plan to go to the north two weeks prior to the trip. In return, North Korean second vice-premier Sŏng-ch'ŏl Park secretly visited Seoul from May 29 to June 1 and met South Korean president Chung-hee Park. These secret missions provided the background of the north-south joint communiqué of July 4, 1972, in which North and South Korea agreed that "a great national unity . . . shall be sought first, transcending differences in ideas, ideologies, and systems." On the basis of this communiqué, the North-South Coordinating Committee was formed on November 4. Full-fledged support for the North-South Red Cross conference to resolve the questions of dispersed families was included in item four of the communiqué.[15]

Meanwhile, the preliminary talks of the North and South Korean Red Cross delegations were concluding, almost one year after they had begun. Agreement over the main talks was finally reached on August 11, 1972.

The first round of the main talks was held at Taedong'gang Hall in P'yŏngyang from August 20 to September 2, 1972. Pŏm-sŏk Lee, chief of the South Korean Red Cross delegation, presided at the opening meeting, which was largely symbolic and ceremonial and conducted in a festive mood. Despite the festivity, the southern delegates were still concerned whether they were there to discuss dispersed families or political issues.

The second round of the main talks took place on September 13 at the Chosun Hotel in Seoul. As the North Korean delegation passed through downtown Seoul for the meeting, citizens of Seoul waved to it in a gesture of genuine welcome. The proceedings were not only broadcast live and unedited but were aired on loudspeakers during the entire conference. The chief of the northern delegation took advantage of this opportunity to make political speeches extolling "Kim Il-sŏng's thoughts." Nationwide resentment was aroused by the political speeches. The South Korean media started criticizing the northern propaganda, and well-informed citizens were deeply disappointed and expressed their concerns about the destiny of the talks.

The mood surrounding the third conference, held in P'yŏngyang from October 23 to 26, 1972, had altered drastically from optimism to despair. The interests of both sides had changed, as had their proposals and counterproposals. The South Korean Red Cross proposed a dialogue about principles to ensure the success of the family search project, but the North Korean delegation demanded the creation of "preconditions." They insisted that "legal conditions should be improved and favorable social circumstances should be created in South Korea." Specifically, North Korea demanded the abrogation of the anticommunist law and the national security law of the south. This session ended in a deadlock.

The stalemate over "improved legal and social conditions in South Korea" continued through the sixth session, which occurred May 8 through 11, 1973. At this session the northern delegation demanded that South Korea "abrogate such anticommunist legislation as the anticommunist law; disband anticommunist agencies and organizations; ban all anticommunist activities; and guarantee the freedom of speech, publication, assembly and movement for people coming from the north to the south to meet their separated families and relatives, provide all kinds of facilities for them and take legal and administrative measures to respect the inviolability of their persons and their belongings."[16]

At the seventh meeting in P'yŏngyang, from July 10 to 13, in an effort to find a breakthrough, the South Korean Red Cross offered a new proposal for the exchange between the north and south of groups visiting ancestors' tombs on the occasion of the 1973 *ch'usŏk*, or harvest festival, holiday on August 15 of the lunar calendar.[17] The proposal was rejected by the north. The seventh round ended without substantive results and without a date set for the eighth round. Seven representatives' meetings and numerous rounds of working-level talks devoted to reviving the main talks followed, but these efforts failed to rescue the talks.

On August 28, 1973, before the opening of the eighth round of Red Cross talks had been decided and after the third session of the North-South Coordinating Committee had been held, North Korea announced its unilateral suspension of the north-south dialogue. North Korea's move brought tension back to the peninsula and ushered in another era of "psychological warfare with infiltration and violence," as Byung Chul Koh termed it in his explanation of Kim's unification policy from 1953 to the late 1960s.[18] The Red Cross conferences between the north and south were not resumed until May 27, 1985.

Incidents of serious violence followed the suspension of talks. On August 15, 1974, South Korea's first lady, Mrs. Park, was assassinated in Japan by a Korean resident there, allegedly a Ch'ongnyŏn member. In November 1974 the first North Korean invasion tunnel beneath the DMZ was discovered.[19] A most bizarre incident occurred in P'anmunjŏm on August 18, 1976, involving two United States army officers. While en route to a tree-pruning detail, they were hacked to death by North Korean soldiers who suddenly ran amok wielding axes and iron bars.

Relations between the north and south in the 1980s have been friendlier, although a major setback occurred with the North Korean terrorist bombing in Rangoon, Burma, on October 9, 1983, which killed several South Korean dignitaries accompanying the president on a state visit.

On September 8, 1984, the North Korean Red Cross offered relief aid, including 7,196 tons of rice, 1,488 bundles of fabric, 759 boxes of medicines, and 100,000 tons of cement, to the thousands of victims in South Korea of one of the worst floods ever recorded there. On September 14 the South Korean Red Cross accepted the north's offer. Subsequently, the North Korean Red Cross delivered the relief items, mobilizing hundreds of trucks and several ships. During the deliveries, two Red Cross officials exchanged ideas about resuming the Red Cross talks, and on November 20 a working-level meeting was held at the truce village of P'anmunjŏm to arrange for the resumption of the plenary session. The two delegations agreed to hold a second meeting at the same place on December 5, but the north postponed it following a shooting incident on November 23 in the joint security area of P'anmunjŏm over the defection to the south by a Russian civilian.

On December 14, however, through the direct telephone line, the North Korean Red Cross agreed to resume full-fledged Red Cross talks in Seoul on January 23, 1985. But on January 9 it notified its counterpart in the south of another indefinite postponement, citing as the reason the joint United States and Republic of Korea military maneuver known as "Team Spirit '85."

Despite the setback caused by the military maneuver, on May 27, 1985, after almost twelve years of no communication, the Red Cross resumed the plenary talks between the north and south in Seoul. Following these talks, a working-level meeting was held in P'anmunjŏm on July 15 at which Red Cross delegates agreed to exchange, sometime in September, folk art troupes and groups wanting to visit their hometowns. The initial proposals made by the two sides were quite different.[20] The North Koreans wanted to restrict all visitors to meeting in Seoul and P'yŏngyang only, while the South Koreans emphasized that visitors should be allowed to go to their hometowns. The north also wanted to allow larger groups than did the south. Compromising on their differences, both sides finally agreed in P'anmunjŏm on August 22 to a simultaneous exchange of a 151-member contingent from each side.[21] Additional talks were held in P'yŏngyang from August 27 to 30. Finally, from September 20 to 23, 1985, these contingents, each consisting of a group leader, fifty dispersed family members, fifty folk singers and dancers, thirty reporters, and twenty support personnel, visited the capital city of the other regime.

This exchange was probably one of the most dramatic events in the history of partitioned Korea, but it had certain limitations. The visits were confined to Seoul and P'yŏngyang; the visitors were not allowed to go to their hometowns. The number of people in the group seeking a reunion with their families was small, and those participating were carefully selected. The list included clergymen, successful businessmen, professors, and an ex-cabinet minister.[22] Twenty of the North Koreans who visited the south and fifteen of the South Koreans who visited the north failed to locate their separated family members. For them, it was a terribly frustrating and sad occasion.

Nevertheless, this event rekindled the fading hopes for the reunion of dispersed families. Sang-hyŏp Kim, ex-prime minister and current president of the South Korean Red Cross, who led the south's contingent to the north, summarized very well the meaning of the exchange upon his arrival in P'yŏngyang. "The current hometown family exchanges are small but this epochmaking event has brightened hopes for expanded exchanges in the future."[23] It is, however, too early to predict the prospects for family reunions among those still separated by the DMZ.

THE REUNION TELETHON, 1983

During their attempts to arrange reunion talks with North Korea in the 1970s, the citizens as well as the government of South Korea learned that there were many obstacles in dealing with the North Koreans. Their words in conferences, at talks, and in communiqués did not necessarily match their actions. Most South Koreans no longer hoped that direct negotiation with the north would produce positive results. In keeping with this realistic assessment following the north-south dialogue, South Koreans tried to make the most of President Park's announcement on June 23, 1973, on what he called foreign policy for peaceful reunification. One hope was to provide the means for separated family members to communicate and meet with each other whenever possible, even with separated family members who were in communist countries.

The South Korean government established mail exchanges with Koreans in Russia, China, Eastern Europe, and other communist countries beginning September 1, 1973. A large number of letters have been sent to and received from Korean residents in Manchuria, Sakhalin Island, and central Asia. Most of the letters have been exchanged between separated family members. A few Korean residents in Manchuria have been able to visit their relatives in South Korea, and some of them have even remained permanently. On March 16, 1975, the Association of the Families of Koreans in China was founded in Seoul for the purpose of bringing home Koreans in China, particularly the elderly and the ill. The association has made contact with 240 families in three northeastern provinces in China. On September 13, 1975, for the first time since World War II, forty Ch'ongnyŏn members (the left-wing organization of Koreans in Japan) entered the Pusan port of South Korea. Since then, the number of visitors has increased annually.

For very complicated legal, political, and financial reasons, it is today difficult for the Korean residents of Sakhalin Island and their relatives in South Korea to visit each other, but correspondence via Japan is possible. Encouraged by the new policy direction of the South Korean government, the South Korean branch of the Society for the Return of Detainees on

Sakhalin was formed in Taegu in 1971 to arrange for an exchange of letters between Koreans on Sakhalin and their relatives in South Korea. This society has also made appeals to the South Korean government, the Japanese government, and the International Committee of the Red Cross for assistance in obtaining the repatriation of the Korean residents on Sakhalin who wished to return to South Korea.

Another manifestation of the renewed efforts to reunite dispersed families was the launching by the South Korean Red Cross on March 31, 1974, of a radio campaign utilizing the Korean Broadcasting System once a week. By February 1976 KBS had broadcast the names of 1,195 people and had reunited 135 families involving 645 individuals. Among the 135 reunions, 17 were between parents and children; 79 were between siblings; 21 were between uncles, aunts, nephews, and nieces; and 13 were between cousins.[24] KBS also broadcast letters being exchanged between Korean residents on Sakhalin and their relatives in South Korea. In response to this program, by February 1976 the volume of letters had increased to 2,500, of which 2,450 were delivered.[25]

The reunion campaign methods of the 1970s continued to be followed into the early 1980s. Efforts to reunite those who were dispersed between the north and south were set aside until the political milieu improved and were instead directed toward reuniting those who were in the south. The major new development in the movement of the early 1980s was the use of modern technology, that is, computers and television. Techniques such as the split screen and simultaneous live broadcasts from different stations nationwide and even from the United States were used with sometimes unexpected results.

Although television had been available in South Korea in the 1960s, it remained largely a luxury item until the late 1970s, particularly in rural regions. This new, powerful mass medium played an important role in the historic reunion telethon in the summer of 1983. It carried messages to an illiterate audience that the print media such as newspapers and magazines were unable to reach.

On June 30, 1983, in the midst of my fieldwork, I stumbled upon a program listing in a morning newspaper for a television special entitled "Yet Lingering Pains of Family Separation during the Korean War." It was scheduled to be telecast live that evening and was to focus on families sundered during the war. This "reunion telethon" was to generate an unprecedented response from the Korean public.

The program was originally scheduled to air for ninety-five minutes and was intended only to describe the pain of sundered family members. But it was so successful in reuniting separated family members by matching them with close-up pictures on the television screen that its impact was instantaneous. Innovative split-screen techniques permitted broadcasters to interconnect many local stations throughout the south and allow simultaneous conversations. Establishing the identities of the seekers and their lost relatives was simplified, even when they were located in different provinces. The potentially related parties could see each other and ask questions by means of the split screen. In most cases a lengthy verification was necessary because the family members had been separated for so long that their memories of one another had faded. In some cases, however, a long verification process was hardly necessary; the viewing audience could easily see the strong resemblance between the two parties.

An elderly woman who appeared on the program had lost her seven-year-old son thirty-three years earlier and could not easily identify him as a forty-year-old middle-aged man. She said that her son had a scar behind one of his ears, the result of an injury by a flying artillery shell during the war. The camera zoomed in to show the scar on the man, instantly confirming that he was the woman's son. An anxious man tried to identify his missing sister by asking many questions, but the woman he was questioning could not answer any of them. They were about to give up when the woman suddenly remembered that there had been two tall pine trees beside a well in front of her family's house in North Korea. The man also remembered the pine trees. Ultimately, they were certain that they were siblings. Television had made their locating and identifying one another possible.

The program generated increasing interest through its success in reuniting families, and anxious people began to flock to the television studio to seek their relatives. The reunion scenes had stimulated the hopes of many separated people, who saw their own chances for reunion rising. This created a snowball effect. KBS found it impossible to end the program at the originally scheduled time because thousands of people had rushed to the studio to register for an appearance before the camera. Finally, KBS made an unprecedented decision to extend the reunion telethon and to cancel other regularly scheduled programs. As the telethon continued, even more people came to the studio. The program stayed on throughout the night, without commercial interruption.

On that first night, after filling out temporary application forms and lining up on a first-come first-served basis, people were allowed to appear on camera for fifteen seconds at a time. Each carried a placard inscribed with his or her own name, the names of the missing persons being sought, and a brief description of how they had been separated. Announcers read the placards while the camera zoomed in on the faces of the searchers. Several telephone lines were open, awaiting inquiries from viewers who thought they were being sought or who recognized the placard bearers. Two announcers worked all through the night, and all the producers devoted their programming efforts entirely to the reunion telethon. The fifteen telephone lines were kept busy handling 1,905 calls.[26]

The reunion telethon was remarkably successful. It reunited many dispersed family members, with the number of reunions increasing as the telethon continued. On June 30, 1983, the first day of the telethon, my field notes indicate that of 850 individuals who appeared on television, 36 (4.2 percent) were reunited with dispersed family members. During the second and third days, July 1 and 2, a total of 268 (6.2 percent) were reunited with their separated members out of 4,300 applicants who were on the program. On July 3, because of the nationwide publicity that had been generated, the rate was drastically increased; of 1,256 applicants, 238 were reunited with relatives, and the reunion rate surpassed 18 percent. The reunion rate steadily increased on the fifth and sixth days. By July 5, its sixth day, the telethon's overall average rate of reuniting family members among the registered people was over 11 percent, even including the first two days that had had a rather low reunion rate because the program was not then as fully publicized. The rate was much higher than anticipated.

Because KBS could not deal with the large number of reunion registrants, the South Korean government committed its support to the telethon, and the South Korean Red Cross organized volunteer workers to assist in the campaign. On July 9, the government announced a comprehensive support program that would coordinate KBS, the Red Cross, and the provisional offices of the five North Korean provinces in South Korea. The government mobilized its administrative units throughout South Korea, including in remote regions, to accept applications for reunion seekers from all over the south and even instructed its embassies throughout the world to accept applications from Koreans living abroad. Many South Korean civic and religious organizations also committed themselves to the cause. The flood of applicants sparked a pan-national movement to assist the telethon.

In response to the overwhelming demand from every quarter of South Korea and after running for a total of sixty-five hours over the first eight

Members of sundered families appear on television during the reunion telethon by KBS in the summer of 1983. Each searcher, who could be on for only fifteen seconds, carries a placard inscribed with his or her name and the names of the persons they are seeking. Courtesy of Dong-A Ilbo.

days, the telethon became a regularly scheduled program every Friday. It became by far the most popular television program in the history of Korean broadcasting, commanding as much as 78 percent of the viewing audience. This regular program continued until November 14, 1983, airing four-and-one-half months with 450 hours of air time. The telethon reunited more than 10,000 persons with sundered family members.

There were negative aspects to the telethon, despite its obvious value; promotional publicity could not be eliminated. To advertise its success, KBS allocated precious air time to the reunion scenes, sometimes as much as ten minutes to one family. In contrast, the searchers were limited to fifteen seconds each on the screen. A camera followed one excited man who had been reunited with his sister as he shouted, "KBS *mansae* [long live KBS]" and "Destroy the puppet regime of North Korea and Il-sŏng Kim." Yet no additional time was given to an eighty-year-old woman who desperately tried to lift her shaking arms a little higher than others in the hope that she could gain a few more seconds of television to find her son. For the

Posters with the names of missing kin displayed outside the KBS studio during the reunion telethon. Courtesy of Dong-A Ilbo.

*A woman anxiously waiting for her appearance on television
to search for her siblings displays a handmade picket sign.
Courtesy of* Dong-A Ilbo.

one-thousandth family reunion KBS appeared to have carefully selected
a particular family who could propagandize the accomplishments of the
South Korean government, including the telethon and its strong anticommunist stand, and condemn the North Korean communists.[27] (KBS is
owned and operated by the South Korean government.)

To gain firsthand experience, I decided to volunteer for the telethon
rather than remain an armchair anthropologist in a hotel room with a television set. The Red Cross let me help at the registration desks that were set

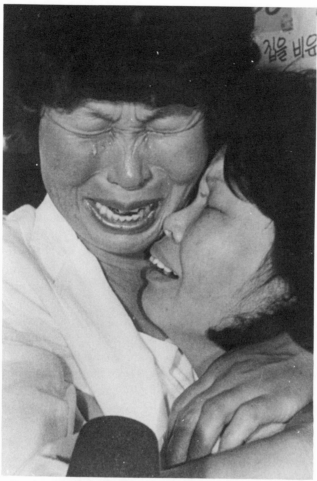

During the reunion telethon, two sisters are reunited on the stairway of the KBS studio after other searchers suggest that they might be related because of their strong resemblance to each other. Courtesy of Dong-A Ilbo.

up in a huge, open square in front of the KBS studio where the reunion telethon was taking place. I was given a Red Cross badge, which gave me free access to every registration desk.

July is the monsoon season in Korea, but the thousands of applicants disregarded the heavy rain as they waited for the Red Cross volunteers, including students from various colleges and universities in Seoul, to assist them in registering for the telethon. The students' services were essential, because so many of those who wished to register were illiterate and could not fill out the application blanks by themselves. This unfortunately helped prolong the application process. It did not take me long to deduce why the previous newspaper campaigns to reunite dispersed family members had not been very successful: many of the separated Koreans could not read.

My involvement in the registration process and my observation of the reunion telethon allowed me to draw some conclusions about the participants. Most seemed to be uneducated, impoverished, and underprivileged. Many were illiterate. Because large numbers had spent their early years in orphanages, many were unable to give their actual ages or exact birth dates or even the names given them by their parents. Most of them bore injuries or scars resulting from the war. Some had gash wounds as a result of being hit by pieces of bombshells or artillery. Some had lost fingers from frostbite after having braved the bitter Korean winter weather as refugees during the retreat that followed the entry of China into the war in 1950–1951. Many had traces of smallpox on their faces, a good indication of the poor sanitation, the lack of preventive vaccine, and the shortage of medicine during the war years.

Some well-to-do Seoulites who watched the telethon were amazed to see such underprivileged Koreans. Wan-sŏ Park, a writer, pointed out that the visages of the people who appeared on television during the reunion telethon might be the true images of the majority of Koreans.[28] The comments of several officials from the provisional offices of the five North Korean provinces indicated their concurrence with my observation: "Most well-established people had already been successful in finding missing family members, at least those living in the south, using other available means. The people who depended solely on this telethon were mostly poor, undereducated, if educated at all, and at the bottom of the socioeconomic structure of contemporary Korean society. Until this telethon began, they had not known of a way to look for their missing family members."

Knowing that a good many of these helpless searchers were anxious to appear on television as soon as possible, some of the "volunteers" took money from them, charging outrageous prices to fill out their forms for them. Many paid the price, so great was their desperation.

One hundred nine thousand applicants registered with the South Korean Red Cross between July 13 and July 31, 1983. People could register with any government administrative unit or any Red Cross office or branch in South Korea and with embassies overseas. Applicants were classified by their home provinces and then listed alphabetically in books that have been made available by the South Korean Red Cross to anyone who desires to search for separated family members. In addition, copies of these records have been distributed to the Korean embassies throughout the world, although for security reasons they cannot be taken from the premises. The South Korean government worries that the North Koreans could use them for espionage purposes. The record books were not available for my fieldwork in the summer of 1984, but during my follow-up field trip to Seoul in December 1984, the South Korean Red Cross shared a statistical analysis of the 109,000 registrants with me, which is summarized in tables 2, 3, and 4 below.

TABLE 2
Distribution of the Red Cross Registrants
by the Year of Their Dispersal

Year of Dispersal	Number of Registrants	Percent (%)
Before 1945	3,333	3.1
1945–1946	16,742	15.3
1947–1948	8,267	7.6
1949–1950*	41,735	38.3
1951–1952*	28,246	25.9
1953*	2,379	2.2
After 1953	1,843	1.7
Unknown	6,455	5.9
Total	109,000	100.0

SOURCE: Prepared by the Republic of Korea National Red Cross.
*During the Korean War.

TABLE 3
Distribution of the Red Cross Registrants by Age

Age	Number of Registrants	Percent (%)
30 and younger	2,321	2.1
31–40	10,865	10.0
41–50	23,737	21.8
51–60	39,186	36.0
61–70	24,033	22.0
71 and older	8,345	7.7
Unknown	513	0.4
Total	109,000	100.0

SOURCE: Prepared by the Republic of Korea National Red Cross.

TABLE 4
Distribution of the Red Cross Registrants
by Relative Being Sought

Relative Being Sought	Number of Registrants	Percent (%)
Parent or child	45,337	24.6
Sibling	79,847	43.3
Spouse	4,927	2.7
Other relative	54,147	29.4
Total	184,258	100.0

SOURCE: Prepared by the Republic of Korea National Red Cross.
NOTE: The total number of registrants is greater than 109,000 because individuals who registered seeking parents as well as siblings were counted two or more times.

According to the analysis of the Red Cross registrants by the year of their dispersal, the largest number (72,360, or 66.4 percent) had been separated from their family members during the Korean War; the next largest number (25,009, or 22.9 percent) had been dispersed from their family members between World War II and the Korean War; a small number had been sundered from their family members before 1945 (3,333, or 3.1 percent) and after the Korean War (1,843, or 1.7 percent); and 6,455 registrants (5.9 percent) did not know when they had been separated from their family members (table 2).

In terms of age distribution of the applicants, 21.8 percent were forty-one to fifty years of age; 36.0 percent were fifty-one to sixty; 22.0 percent were sixty-one to seventy; 7.7 percent were seventy-one and older; and 12.1 percent were forty years old and younger. Most of the applicants were thus middle-aged (table 3).

In terms of the distribution of the Red Cross registrants by relative being sought, most of the registrants (43.3 percent) were looking for siblings; 24.6 percent were searching for parents or children; only 2.7 percent were seeking reunions with spouses; and 29.4 percent of the registrants were seeking cousins, uncles and aunts, or other relatives (table 4).

Few of the registrants were searching for spouses, and few of these were reunited with them, but this does not mean that there were fewer cases of dispersed spouses than of other family members. There is an indication that, although most remarried individuals may have wanted to rejoin their former spouses, they stayed away from the reunion telethon to avoid creating strains in their current marriages. Even when the current spouse knows that his or her mate has been married previously and is understanding, any effort to locate the first spouse tends to make the current spouse unhappy. Locating the first spouse would also create a polygamous situation.

During the reunion telethon, I met a university professor who had fled south during the war, leaving his wife and a daughter in the north. He had eventually remarried in the south. He told me that he would not seek his first wife and said that he did not even watch the program because he was afraid of what he might do and kept himself occupied to avoid watching the television. "I like my life as it is now. Trying to locate my first wife would create a difficult situation," he said. I was told that many who were in the same position as the professor went to bars to drink. Some solved the problem differently. A sixty-year-old man who was seeking his brother-in-law revealed: "Actually I'm trying to find my former wife, but if I locate my brother-in-law, then he might know about his sister and what happened to her."

It is perhaps too early to speculate about potential problems resulting from the reunions. These will probably warrant a separate study later. But many difficulties have already started to surface. The joy and excitement of meeting a long-lost relative may last for a few days or perhaps a few weeks, but longer-term economic, social, and psychological effects on the reunited families are being left unattended, posing a potential social problem for Korean society. The reunions seem to create disequilibrium in the existing family units. For example, segments of the separated family units that are better off financially seem to be held responsible, as patrons, for the segments that are not so well off.

From April 1 through May 25, 1984, a team of social surveyors from Korea University and the *Hankook Ilbo* newspaper studied the adjustment problems of reunited families. An analysis of a sample of 336 families revealed that only a few reunited family members were living together (2.1 percent) and that among the others contact was less frequent than expected: 74.1 percent met once a month, but 9.3 percent met less than once a month or irregularly, and 14.5 percent had had no contact since their reunions. Most of those surveyed wanted to get together on occasions such as weddings and funerals but were reluctant to engage in any monetary transaction.[29]

A few tragic incidents were also attributed to the telethon. On the fourth day of the telethon a seventy-one-year-old North Korean refugee, Kwang-sil Park, hung himself in a pine tree behind his house after watching the telethon and becoming frustrated about his situation. He left a short note to his son, his child by a woman he had married in the south. Kwang-sil had fled North Korea alone, leaving his wife and six sons and three daughters there. Although there was but a slim chance that his former wife and his nine children would be living in the south, he could not bear the thought of carrying a placard with their names in front of the camera because he was afraid of hurting the feelings of his current wife and son. He found it intolerable, however, to do nothing at all while watching others being reunited with their separated family members. Finally, to escape the dilemma, he chose to commit suicide.[30]

On the fifth day of the telethon, another North Korean refugee, fifty-nine-year-old Wŏn-jo Kim, who had fled south leaving his parents and siblings in the north, committed suicide by taking an overdose of sleeping pills while watching the telethon. Another death occurred when a resident of Pusan, sixty-five-year-old Chun-sŏk Chŏn, who had also left his parents and siblings in the north, had a stroke while watching the reunion program; he died after being taken to the hospital.[31]

In general, however, the reunion telethon was considered a great success. Several factors contributed to this success including not only the key personnel who created and put on the telethon but also the social conditions of contemporary Korea. First, credit must be given to the overall improvement of the Korean economy. In 1983, thirty years after the Korean War, South Korea was enjoying an era of sustained, rapid economic growth. South Korea's economic achievements are reflected in impressive statistics regarding annual growth in its GNP, which grew at the annual rate of 6.9% during 1960 to 1978. Per capita income increased from about one hundred dollars to fifteen hundred dollars per year in one generation.[32] Exports, which had accounted for only about 2 percent of the GNP in 1960, had reached 28 percent of a vastly expanded GNP by 1975.[33] Korean living standards had improved tremendously. Television became available to ordinary citizens. By the early 1980s almost every household, both in rural and urban areas, had a television set. Such universal access to television supported the KBS endeavor.

Second, technological innovations in the television industry, such as split-screen imaging, also contributed to the telethon's success. Robert H. Lauer's point that technological change has multiple effects was aptly illustrated by the reunion telethon.[34] Moreover, by 1983 KBS had grown and added many affiliated local stations. There were twenty-two local stations, nine of which participated in the simultaneous live telecasts of the telethon.

Third, an indirect contribution was made by the overall change in the attitude of Koreans toward reunion with dispersed family members, a change that began with the proposal of Red Cross talks between north and south on August 12, 1971. The political dialogue between North and South Korea and the subsequent announcement of the north-south joint communiqué on July 4, 1972; the open-door policy announced June 23, 1973, to allow mail exchange with Korean residents in communist countries; and the invitation of September 13, 1975, extended to procommunist Korean residents in Japan to visit South Korea all contributed to the growing optimism. Although the talks and dialogue did not produce concrete results, they helped to eliminate psychological barriers. Even though the talks were limited to a few privileged delegates, such an exchange between the north and south fostered the hope that the reunion of sundered families could be achieved.

In the summer of 1983, when the reunion telethon was experiencing its remarkable success in reuniting separated families, Prime Minister Sanghyŏp Kim (formerly a university professor), spoke apologetically during a visit to the KBS studio: "It is regrettable for us in government not to have done this simple thing sooner."[35] Many in the viewing audience, touched by the poignant accounts, shared the prime minister's sentiments. But their regrets exceeded his. "If the government had started such a campaign sooner, more people, especially the elderly, would have had the chance to have been reunited with their relatives before they died": this was a theme dominating conversations during the early weeks of the telethon. As the media began to report worldwide the dramatic reunion event, Koreans everywhere were jubilant. At the same time, many of them felt guilt, shame, and annoyance because of the ineptness of their government, which had done very little to reunite dispersed family members during the preceding thirty years.

Their regrets and frustration were based mainly on the fact that the dispersal of so many families had occurred wholly within the south. Many people had been unable to be reunited with separated members simply because of the absence of a mechanism to bring them together. The government seemed to mobilize all its resources only to search for unattainable goals. Identifying and finding missing family members in the south did not need the approval of the North Koreans. One foreign reporter following the telethon made the cynical comment, "There could be no harsher criticism than this occasion to prove the incompetence of the governments under the different leaderships."[36]

North Koreans also recognize the anguish of families separated during the war. According to the observations of a group of Korean-American political scientists who visited P'yŏngyang in the summer of 1981, tales of family separation during the war are common on television just as South Korean television series have depicted the sagas of dispersed families. Sung Chul Yang, who was one of the six-member team who visited North Korea, reported his observations at the Children's Palace in P'yŏngyang: "In another room I saw a skit dramatizing the sorrows and tragedy of separated families—a granddaughter in the North longed for reunion with her grandmother in the South, whom she had never met; she did not even know whether the grandmother was still alive."[37] The North Korean government, however, has not taken any specific steps to ease the pain of those suffering from separation.

CHAPTER 8
Reunited Families

The KBS reunion telethon created an ideal laboratory for my intensive fieldwork as the hundreds and thousands of dispersed Koreans gathered together in Yŏido Square for their television appearances. Participating as a Red Cross volunteer in registering people for the telethon, I helped, observed, and even wept with the dispersed family members.

The following accounts of reunited family members are based on my field notes taken during the telethon and on reports published in newspapers and magazines. Additional information on each of the families included in this chapter was obtained from interviews conducted by seven *Dong-A Ilbo* newspaper reporters on special assignment. The *Dong-A Ilbo* permitted me to incorporate information from the interviews into my field notes. Without this assistance, I would have been able to document only what I observed in Yŏido Square and what I watched on television. At the time, it would have been impossible for me to trace any of the thousands of reunited families while I was helping at the registration desks. In addition, the newspaper reporters had had access to the KBS studio, whereas I had not been allowed to go beyond the registrations desks.

The reunion telethon in addition to reuniting families directly also helped reunite dispersed Koreans indirectly through other media. The involvement of a newspaper and a computerized identification system was also successful in bringing together dispersed family members, as were posters and signs displayed by the thousands of waiting registrants.

SPOUSES REUNITED BY TELEVISION

Among the reunion telethon applicants who registered to search for family members, only a limited number were trying to locate spouses, and few of these people were reunited with their husbands or wives by the telethon. The first such reunion did not occur until the eighteenth day of the telethon, and was a great event not only for the reunited parties but also for the millions of viewers.

At five o'clock in the afternoon on July 17, 1983, on the eighteenth day of the reunion telethon at the KBS studio, sixty-three-year-old Pong-ju Park was dramatically reunited with his sixty-one-year-old wife, Sae-ran Kim; it was the first time they had seen one another since they had been separated thirty-three years before at a refugee camp in Seoul. They were happy and excited, as they wept together at the moment of their reunion. Nevertheless, they were no longer the young couple they had been, and both were remarried.

Pong-ju and Sae-ran were both originally from P'yŏngyang in North Korea. They had married shortly before the outbreak of the Korean War. When the war began, the newlywed couple decided to flee to the south. They managed to get to Seoul and stayed most of the time in a refugee camp set up on the grounds of an elementary school. They did not have anyplace else to go, having no relatives or friends in Seoul. There Sae-ran gave birth to a daughter, whom they named Myŏng-suk.

When Myŏng-suk was three months old, Pong-ju was drafted by the South Korean army and was forced to leave his wife and daughter in the temporary refugee camp. The camp was relocated many times as the South Korean army retreated southward, and during the commotion of the war, Pong-ju and his wife lost contact with one another.

When the war ended, Pong-ju was discharged from military duty. He searched for his family everywhere, for one full year visiting every refugee camp, but he was unable to find his wife and daughter. Giving up at last, Pong-ju remarried in 1954 and settled down in Ch'ŏngju in Ch'ungch'ŏng Puk-do province, working as a carpenter. He and his second wife, now fifty-six years old, had two sons and two daughters. They live comfortably in Ch'ŏngju.

After Pong-ju had been sent to the front, Sae-ran and Myŏng-suk had a difficult time surviving in their crude environment. Owing to the lack of supplies, many of the refugees in the camp suffered from malnutrition. At times, Sae-ran's body became swollen because of the limited quantity and poor quality of the food available to her. Sae-ran and Myŏng-suk transferred from one refugee camp to another. They ended up far south in Iri in Chŏlla Nam-do province, in the southwestern part of the peninsula.

After South Korea recaptured Seoul, Sae-ran and her daughter moved back to the city. Not knowing that Pong-ju was looking for her, Sae-ran blamed her husband for abandoning her and their child. She took any available work in the different marketplaces in Seoul to support herself and her young daughter.

Despite her hardships, for years she never gave serious consideration to remarrying, and she managed to raise Myŏng-suk alone. In 1976, after twenty-six difficult years, Myŏng-suk married, and Sae-ran lost her closest companion. Myŏng-suk was everything to Sae-ran, and she became very lonely after her daughter's marriage. Even though Sae-ran resisted the idea, Myŏng-suk begged her mother to remarry for companionship. In 1978, by arrangement of her daughter, Sae-ran married a sixty-nine-year-old man. He was also a North Korean refugee who had fled south alone during the war, leaving his wife and son in Hamkyŏng Puk-do province in North Korea. As refugees with similar backgrounds, they found they had many things in common and could understand each other very well. They have been good companions in marriage.

During the reunion telethon, as many dispersed family members were being reunited, Pong-ju could not simply sit and watch. He felt compelled to do something about locating his wife and daughter, unable to go on without at least trying to find out about them. Finally, Pong-ju called his family together to tell them about his past, and he asked for their understanding and support. Pong-ju's current wife was quite sympathetic with her husband and gave full approval to his search for his former wife and daughter. His children were also supportive. Encouraged by their understanding, Pong-ju registered at the Ch'ŏngju KBS station, and that very afternoon he appeared on television as a reunion seeker.

Sae-ran never dreamed that Pong-ju would be on the reunion telethon. But since she was one of the many North Koreans who had been separated from family members during the war, she could not help but watch the telethon. To her amazement, on the afternoon of July 16, she saw her first husband, Pong-ju, from whom she had been severed for thirty-three years.

There he was, looking for her and her daughter, Myŏng-suk. When she saw him, she felt mixed emotions of love and hatred. Momentarily, she forgot about her current position. She called her daughter immediately and told her that her father was looking for them. Sae-ran did not know what to do then, but Myŏng-suk insisted that her mother call KBS and notify them right away. She did so without thinking of the complications that could develop. KBS arranged for Pong-ju to come to the studio in Seoul for their reunion. He came accompanied by his twenty-five-year-old son, one of his four children by the wife he had in the south.

At first, Pong-ju and Sae-ran seemed tense and stiff. They looked awkwardly at each other. It was impossible to guess what thoughts were going through their minds. They could not speak but could only cry together. This touching scene caused everyone who witnessed it to weep with them. Their story was not just the tragedy of one family. It symbolized the historical calamity that had affected all Koreans, the fratricidal war that had resulted from the clash of forces greater than Korea itself.

Chae-ho, Pong-ju's son, said with tears in his eyes, "I feel like I have another mother, and I intend to treat her like my own mother." Thirty-eight-year-old Myŏng-suk, the only child of Pong-ju and Sae-ran, wept as she said frankly, "Since my father and I were separated from each other when I was only three months old, in all honesty I cannot really feel any love for him as my father. But, I am thrilled to death to find him."

The reunited couple went to their daughter's apartment in Seoul after their television appearance. Myŏng-suk also invited her half-brother Chae-ho. Pong-ju and Sae-ran did not reveal to interviewers what they discussed there, but most likely they attempted to catch up on what had happened to each of them during their long separation. After that first evening at Myŏng-suk's apartment, Sae-ran introduced her seventy-four-year-old second husband to Pong-ju, and Pong-ju took Sae-ran and Myŏng-suk to Ch'ŏngju and introduced them to his current wife. Pong-ju repeatedly said, "It was just a tragedy, a tragedy, and a tragedy. That's all I can say."

The thrilling reunion between these two sundered spouses raises potentially complicated problems that have to be solved. It remains to be seen what Pong-ju and Sae-ran will do. It is not at issue whether their second marriages were illegal or unethical. At the same time, however, is Pong-ju responsible for Sae-ran when her second husband dies? Prevailing Korean mores do not offer guidelines for appropriate or simple solutions to such questions.

REUNIONS THROUGH THE NEWSPAPER

The reunion of Pong-ju and Sae-ran was to some extent due to luck. If Sae-ran had not continued to watch the reunion telethon so intently, she could easily have missed seeing her first husband. In order to accommodate as many applicants as possible, the telethon ran without interruption, not even for station breaks, and the time allocated for each individual's appearance on camera was kept short. During the early stages of the telethon, some families mobilized all of their members to take turns watching it, even keeping their children home from school to watch for the names of missing family members who might appear.

To offset the weaknesses of the television format and to assist those who were unable to watch television continuously, the *Hankook Ilbo* newspaper published a special daily extra edition that listed the names and gave brief descriptions of the people who appeared on the telethon each day, along with the names of those they were seeking. The *Hankook Ilbo* distributed the extra free of charge. It allowed people the opportunity to peruse the information at length instead of hastily viewing images on a television screen. The newspaper helped significantly in reuniting hundreds of dispersed family members, including more than ten cases of Koreans overseas.

An overseas edition (also published in Los Angeles and New York City) of the *Hankook Ilbo*, *The Korea Times Chicago Edition*, also put out a special edition listing the applicants for the reunion telethon. Forty-nine-year-old Tong-hwa Hŏ, a Korean resident of Chicago, found the name of her forty-four-year-old brother, Yong-gu, in the list. Tong-hwa thought her brother had died during the war, and he was recorded as dead in her family register. She also found her two other siblings. Fifty-six-year-old Ha-jin Lee, who lives in Los Angeles, was reunited with her forty-six-year-old sister, Suk-ja, who lives in Ch'ŏngwŏn in Ch'ungch'ŏng Puk-do province.

The reunion of Yong-jun Kim and his wife Chŏng-hi Noh was made possible by the *Hankook Ilbo's* special edition in South Korea. Yong-jun, Chŏng-hi, and their two children had lived in Sakju in P'yŏngan Nam-do province in North Korea before the war. Their life in Sakju had been comfortable. During the war, however, as the United Nations and South Korean forces retreated from occupied North Korea in the winter of 1950, they considered fleeing south. Twenty-six-year-old Yong-jun wanted his

wife to leave before the communist troops recaptured Sakju. Chŏng-hi
was, however, reluctant to abandon her home. She thought that her husband and their nine-year-old son, Sun-t'ae, should go so that the heir of
the family would be safe. There was no time to argue about who should go
and who should remain. Yong-jun and Sun-t'ae finally left for the south,
leaving Chŏng-hi and their five-year-old daughter, Sun-ja, in Sakju.

After Yong-jun and Sun-t'ae left, Chŏng-hi changed her mind. She was
afraid to stay behind, alone with only a five-year-old daughter, especially
in view of rumors that the Chinese soldiers would rape Korean women.
She decided to go to South Korea taking Sun-ja, hoping that she would
find her husband and son in Seoul. It was a naive hope. She thought Seoul
would be like the small town of Sakju, but the great city was overflowing
with tens of thousands of refugees crowded into temporary camps. She
was unable to find Yong-jun and Sun-t'ae.

Instead of remaining in Seoul, Yong-jun and Sun-t'ae had settled in the
small town of P'ung'gi in Kyŏngsang Puk-do province in the southeastern
section of the peninsula. Later, Yong-jun remarried there, and Chŏng-hi
gave up her search, finally remarrying in Seoul. Ironically, by the time of
the reunion telethon, both had been widowed and were again single.

Both hesitated to participate in the telethon because of their second
marriages. But Sun-t'ae, now forty-two, was eager to search for his separated mother, on the chance that she and his sister were in the south. He
registered for the telethon on its second day but received no response. For
several days Sun-t'ae wandered around the KBS studio and the vicinity of
the telethon reading the wall posters in hopes that either his mother or
sister were looking for him or his father. After much searching, he gave up
hope that they had ever come south at all.

Meanwhile, Sun-ja, a thirty-eight-year-old housewife and a regular sub-
scriber of the *Hankook Ilbo*, was carefully checking the lists of telethon registrants. She could not watch television on the night her brother was on,
but she did find his name in the special edition of the *Hankook Ilbo*. She
called Sun-t'ae right away, and the brother and sister spoke to one another
for the first time in thirty years. Sun-t'ae relayed the thrilling news to his
father in P'ung'gi immediately, and the four dispersed family members
were finally reunited in Seoul.

Sun-t'ae insisted that his parents live together with him in Seoul. Because their second spouses were deceased, there was no impediment to
reuniting if they wanted to. Also, their situation raised fewer issues than
that of many other reunited couples. It remains to be seen, however, what

problems Yong-ju and Chŏng-hi might have adjusting to one another after so long a separation.

A WALL POSTER REUNITES A FAMILY

Because of the high turnout for the telethon, the lines grew long, and the registrants became impatient as they waited their turn to appear on television. They started to paste their own homemade posters on every available space: on walls, on the sidewalks, on parked vans, and even on their bodies. The posters were inscribed with their names, the names of the missing, and brief descriptions of how they had been separated from the missing family member. Some people displayed picket signs. Others floated balloons in the air with their posters hanging from them to draw attention to them. Although no one counted the families who were re-united by means of the signs and wall posters, a good many people were able to locate family members this way. It was not as inefficient a means as it might seem, since many of the anxious searchers remained near the KBS studio. To bring order to the chaotic display of posters and pickets during the telethon, the government finally constructed a temporary hall for them in Yŏido Square near the KBS studio. It stayed open for eleven months, until June 30, 1984.

A wall poster reunited fifty-two-year-old Nak-ki Lee with his father and a sister. He registered with the telethon to search for his separated parents and siblings, but, like others, he had to wait many hours before his ap-pearance. He became so impatient that, like thousands of other people, he made a poster. It read:

Lost family members: Father, Chong-chik (77); Mother, San-hwa; Siblings, Nak-hong, Ch'ang-ho, Yŏng-suk, and Ch'ang-hun.
Hometown: Saman-ri, Pakch'ŏn, P'yŏngan Puk-do province.
Separation: Separated from mother and three brothers near the Sŏnkyo-ri railroad station in P'yŏngyang during the retreat of December 1950; separated from father and sister, Yŏng-suk, in Taebang-dong, Seoul.
Name of searcher: Nak-ki Lee.

Nak-ki also decided that contacting the provisional office of P'yŏngan Puk-do, which during the telethon had a temporary office in a tent at Yŏido Square, might give him a better chance of locating his family mem-bers. After he filed his application at the P'yŏngan Puk-do office, Nak-ki started reading the seemingly endless array of wall posters and picket signs.

He read them one by one, enduring the pouring July monsoon rain and without stopping for meals, until he was exhausted. At ten o'clock in the morning, on the day he was to appear on the telethon, Nak-ki heard a voice over the loudspeaker: the P'yŏngan Puk-do office was paging him. The office staff had found another picketer who was looking for the same individuals as on Nak-ki's list. The two posters both listed Chong-chik Lee as father. The excited Nak-ki dashed to the office and met there a young man holding a list with the name of his father. Nak-ki asked him, "Who is this man to you?" pointing to the name of his father. The young man replied, "He is my father, and my name is Nak-kyo." Nak-ki was unaware of the existence of this brother. Nak-kyo asked Nak-ki, "What is your name, and what is your relationship to my father?" "My name is Nak-ki, and Chong-chik is also my father," replied Nak-ki. Nak-ki and Nak-kyo turned out to be half-brothers. Nak-kyo had been born to Chong-chik by a second wife in the south. Nak-ki asked his half-brother, "Why didn't you include my name in your list?" Nak-kyo was astonished to discover his eldest brother. "I heard that you were killed in action during the war." Nak-ki grumbled, "I didn't die. Here I am. Who told you that?" Nak-kyo did not know how to respond.

Nak-ki learned that his father had remarried in the south and was living in P'yŏngt'aek and that his younger sister, Yŏng-suk, who had been only five years old when he was separated from her in a Seoul street in the winter of 1950, was now a middle-aged housewife living in Seoul. After a phone call from Nak-kyo, Yŏng-suk hurried to Yŏido Square to be reunited with her brother. Yŏng-suk explained to Nak-ki the reason why they had not included his name in the search list. In 1966 the family was notified by the South Korean army that Nak-ki had been killed in action during the war. The family had even been receiving his death pensions from the government twice a year. She also told Nak-ki that their mother and the rest of their siblings were still missing. She thought they were probably still in North Korea. Immediately after the reunion with his half-brother and his sister, Nak-ki and his wife went with them to P'yŏngt'aek to see his now ailing father.

Nak-ki was the eldest child, among four boys and one girl, of Chong-chik Lee, a yeoman farmer who made a comfortable living for his family but fortunately was not classified as one of the landlords who would be expelled from the village. The family did not have any problems even under communist rule. But when the war broke out, most of the youngsters were mobilized, nineteen-year-old Nak-ki among them. He was sent to

Chŏngju to be trained before being sent to the front. He managed to run away from the Chŏngju training center and came home. He was sent to a mountain hideaway with his cousins until the United Nations and South Korean forces captured his hometown.

His freedom did not last long. When the United Nations and the South Korean forces began retreating southward, his family decided to flee to the south, going by way of P'yŏngyang to join the family of his uncle in P'yŏngyang. In early December 1950 the entire family left their Saman-ri home. Nak-ki's mother carried two-year-old Ch'ang-hun on her back, and his father carried five-year-old Yŏng-suk on the top of their luggage. The other children walked to P'yŏngyang. Their journey took nearly ten days. As they reached the outskirts of P'yŏngyang, there were frequent bombings, and they had to seek shelter often. So many people were pouring into the streets that it was difficult for Nak-ki and his family to stay together. Because they all knew the location of their uncle's home, they decided they would meet there if they were forced to take separate routes. This plan seemed reasonable at the time, but it turned out to be ineffective when the family did get dispersed in the crowd. Nak-ki arrived alone near his uncle's home in P'yŏngyang, but he could not find the house. Bombings had completely destroyed that section of the city. His uncle had not been able to wait for Nak-ki and his family after the retreat of the United Nations and South Korean forces from P'yŏngyang on December 4.

Wandering around the Sŏnkyo-ri railroad station in the suburbs of P'yŏngyang, Nak-ki fortunately came upon his father and Yŏng-suk, but they had lost contact with his mother and three brothers. Nak-ki, his father, and Yŏng-suk looked for the others everywhere, but they could not find them. They were unable to wait for them long, and reluctantly, the three retreated southward, following other refugees.

They got to Seoul despite the many obstacles they faced on their journey, but once there they had no place to go. Nak-ki was anxious to go back to find the missing four family members. He decided that one sure way to return to the north would be to join the South Korean army and be assigned to duty at the front. When Nak-ki first volunteered, the army turned him down because of his poor health. He was near starvation and had suffered from diarrhea during the long and miserable journey as a refugee, and he could not meet the minimum weight requirement. The army referred him to the national guard, but this assignment did not satisfy him because he would not be sent to the front line. Meanwhile, Nak-ki was once again separated from his family. He had left his father and sister in the streets of Taebang-dong in Seoul and was unable to find them after he returned from the army recruiting office.

Nak-ki persisted in his effort to become a regular soldier until he finally succeeded in joining the regular army in 1952. His division did not have a chance to march to the north, where he could have looked for his missing mother and three brothers. The war reached a stalemate, and while he was stationed south of the thirty-eighth parallel, the truce agreement was signed. His dreams of revisiting his hometown of Saman-ri and searching for his mother and brothers had to be relinquished.

Nak-ki was discharged from military duty in January 1954. He did not have any place to go nor anyone to whom he could turn. He took menial jobs in construction, mining, and other areas, none of which lasted very long. The South Korean economy right after the war was unable to provide work for the young men who were discharged from their military duties. Eventually he became a salesman for a pharmaceutical company, when better jobs became available in the mid-1960s and the 1970s as the Korean economy improved. He married a woman from Yŏngpyŏn, which adjoined his home county of P'yŏngan Puk-do province in North Korea.

Nak-ki admitted that "In all honesty, while I was struggling to find work and worrying about my next meal, I did not have the peace of mind to look for my family. Frankly, I was preoccupied with how I could manage myself. I began attempting to find my father and the rest of my family after I got my current job and was married. From then on, I often visited the offices of the associations of the citizens of P'yŏngan Puk-do. I attended the gatherings of the fellowships and other events. At those meetings I met my second cousins and some old hometown friends and acquaintances. But nobody seemed to know about my family. I became deeply frustrated."

Assuming that his parents both had passed away, Nak-ki observed ancestor worship rites for them. These rites are usually observed on the anniversaries of the ancestors' deaths, but since Nak-ki did not know the dates on which his parents had died, he could only observe the rites on holidays. On every August 15, the day of the *ch'usŏk* or harvest festival and on New Year's Day by the lunar calendar, Nak-ki dutifully observed the ancestor worship rites for his presumably dead father. He did this for ten years unaware that his father was living not far from Seoul.

On their way to visit their father, Yŏng-suk told Nak-ki that she and their father had lived almost like street beggars after they first arrived in P'yŏngt'aek. Chong-chik's life with a five-year-old daughter had been difficult. He had had to do menial chores, the kind the villagers liked to avoid, to maintain a marginal living. When Chong-chik worked in the fields, little Yŏng-suk had to stay by herself. Sympathetic neighbors often gave her something to eat. Gradually, Chong-chik's hard work allowed him to improve their standard of living.

After three years Chong-chik was able to afford decent shelter and to send Yŏng-suk to elementary school. She was eight years old, two years behind most of the other children. Giving up the hope of reuniting with his separated wife, he remarried. Nak-kyo, who went to Seoul for the reunion telethon, was the first child born to Chong-chik and his second wife. Later, they had two more children. Yŏng-suk went to Seoul and worked in a shoe manufacturing company to earn money to help her father, who was struggling to support his new and enlarging family. She sent most of her earnings to P'yŏngt'aek until, at the age of twenty-six, she got married.

The trip to P'yŏnt'aek made by Nak-ki, his wife, and Yŏng-suk was not altogether a cheerful one. They regretted that the rest of their family was still missing. Further, Nak-ki was saddened to hear from his sister that their father had suffered from a stroke five years earlier.

As they neared P'yŏngt'aek, Yŏng-suk said to Nak-ki, "I wonder if father will recognize you." When they arrived at their father's home, Chong-chik met them outside. Yŏng-suk went up to him alone and told her father calmly, "Father, why don't we go inside the house? I have good news to tell you." The seventy-seven-year-old man looked at the middle-aged man and woman and slowly followed his daughter. About ten minutes later, Yŏng-suk called her brother and sister-in-law to come in, saying, "He'll be all right. I told him everything."

The inside of the room seemed dim to Nak-ki and his wife. Nak-ki did not know what to say at first, and his wife felt even more awkward. Finally, Nak-ki said, "Father! This is Nak-ki, your son! I've come back." He and his wife bowed to his father together.

Although Chong-chik seemed gravely ill, he was still alert and had good vision. He remained calm, but he could not believe what was happening. He said, "Nak-ki was very skinny, and his chin was sharp, long, and projected forward." Chong-chik could not believe that this man who had suddenly shown up and who appeared to him to be rather plump was his missing son. Chong-chik's memory of his son had not dimmed, despite the many years that had separated them; it was more accurate than any photograph.

Nak-ki replied, "Yes, I used to be really thin, but lately I've been gaining some weight." His father still could not believe that the son who had been reported dead was still alive and now standing before him. Desperate to find a way to verify his son's identity, Chong-chik sat deeply in thought for a long time. Finally he said, "Nak-ki once broke his chin on an ox-drawn cart." Nak-ki showed his chin to his ailing father: "That's right. I remember that accident—I had to have twenty stitches. Look, you can still see the scars." Chong-chik carefully examined the scars on Nak-ki's face and even touched them. "It's Nak-ki, my son. It's really Nak-ki, no doubt about it," he said. "I didn't think you could still be alive. It's Nak-ki!" The long-lost father and son embraced each other and wept with happiness. No words were needed to express their joy at being reunited after thirty-three years of separation.

REUNION OF SPOUSES
BY COMPUTER IDENTIFICATION

For the purpose of issuing identification cards, the South Korean government registered all its citizens who were seventeen years and older. Twenty-six million people were registered, and the national police headquarters stored all the information so that the data bank could be used for many purposes, including criminal investigations. Beginning in June 1982, one year before the telethon, this data was used to search for family members dispersed during the war.

From June 1982 to June 1983 a total of 7,855 people registered with the police to look for their families. Of the 7,855 registrants, 2,180 were reunited with separated family members, and 1,220 were still actively searching. Because of insufficient information, 4,455 cases were futile. The government's success rate with its computerized matching system was 27.8 percent, substantially higher than the overall reunion rate (11.7 percent) of the KBS reunion telethon.[1] The South Korean government's plan to use the computer to assist the over 200,000 people who registered with KBS and the South Korean Red Cross after the initial television broadcast was based on this success rate.

Despite the success and apparent efficiency of the computer search, however, the method had several problems. First, it had not been well publicized. Even though I was researching this subject, I was unaware of such a mechanism until it was mentioned on the first night of the reunion telethon. Without the announcement that night, few other people would have known of the existence of such a method.

The second problem associated with the computer search was the stigma attached to the Korean police. Most Koreans feel uneasy about visiting police headquarters, as if by doing so they could be associated with criminal activity. In the eyes of most Koreans the police station is where guilty or bad people go. If the computers had been accessible through other organizations, such as the Red Cross, more people would have used them.

A third problem was posed by the limitations of the computer search system itself. These became apparent during the reunion telethon. To use the computer to find missing family members, one had to have fairly accurate personal information, including at least the name and age of an individual. Some people, however, for example many who had been raised in orphanages were unable to supply even these facts. They had been too young when orphaned to remember such specific information. The following two reunion stories illustrate the capabilities and limits of the computer identification system.

During the telethon, thirty-nine-year-old Chong-chin Maeng displayed a rather unusual placard. It read: "Name: Chong-chin Maeng, 39 years old. I am looking for my parents and siblings, but I do not know their names and ages. I cannot even remember how they look. Hometown: P'yŏngt'aek." Chong-chin had been separated from his family in January 1951 near P'yŏngt'aek during a severe bombardment while they were retreating southward. During the commotion, six-year-old Chong-chin became separated from his family and was taken to an orphanage. After the bombardment was over, his parents could not find him. Later, they were told by other refugees that their son had been killed during the bombing raid. The parents could not stay to confirm their son's death. They had to keep moving, assuming that their son, whose real name was Sŏng-man Hong, had been killed. At the orphanage the boy was arbitrarily given a new name.

The family decided, as they were watching the telethon, that Chong-chin Maeng looked like their missing son, Sŏng-man, although the name and hometown he gave were different. They further thought that, although they were from Hwanghae-do province in North Korea, their young son may have only been able to remember P'yŏngt'aek in association with his parents since their separation had taken place at P'yŏngt'aek. Thanks to the computer's power, they were able to start checking available morphological characteristics of Chong-chin; ultimately, they were able to confirm the identity of their missing son by twin whirls of hair on his head and an unusual, misshapen chest. Thus it was that Chong-chin, in searching for his dispersed family, learned that he was really Sŏng-man Hong and that his hometown was Yŏnbaek in North Korea, not P'yŏngt'aek. This incredible match-up with only the benefit of partial information about the individual could not have been accomplished with a computer alone.

Another match-up during the reunion telethon brought together sixty-one-year-old Kwang-yŏn Lee and her forty-year-old son, Sŏng-su Kim, who had officially registered his age as thirty-seven. They had been separated when Kwang-yŏn put six-year-old Sŏng-su on the top of a freight train at Chunghwa railroad station near P'yŏngyang during the winter retreat of 1950. As she turned around to pick up their other belongings, the train left her behind. In the chaos of retreat by the flood of refugees, she could not locate her boy after that. Sŏng-su was subsequently reared in an orphanage, and although he remembered his real name, he was unsure about his age. The orphanage made an intelligent guess, creating a three-year discrepancy. Despite this discrepancy, there was enough accurate information so that the computer could link the mother and son who had been separated thirty-three years earlier in the north.

The computer was indeed the medium for the reunion of sixty-year-old Ch'ang-su Han, and his wife, fifty-five-year-old Ok-ja Park, who had been separated during the second retreat from Seoul in January 1951. They had only been married since the spring of 1950. Before their separation, Ch'ang-su had been working at a United States Army arsenal as a civilian employee. When the army retreated suddenly from Seoul, Ch'ang-su followed without notifying his wife or parents. At the time, his parents were getting ready to leave to move to the rural village where one of their daughters lived; they hoped to avoid the severe bombings and street fighting that was anticipated in Seoul. His wife, Ok-ja, was away, visiting her natal home. Her sister-in-law, Kyŏng-suk, who had once worked at the official residence of the United States military governor in Korea as a waitress, came by with a microbus that had been arranged for her by her former employer to take her and her parents to safety further south. Ok-ja's parents-in-law, however, did not want to leave; they wanted to wait until Ok-ja returned from her visit so they could all go together. But the bus was loaded with people, and it could not wait, for an enemy attack was imminent. And so Ok-ja's parents-in-law and sister-in-law left on the microbus. When Ok-ja returned, she found the house of her parents-in-law deserted and empty, as were the streets of Seoul. She could hear the sounds of artillery fire. She went back to her natal home, having become hopelessly separated from her husband's family.

Ok-ja stayed with her parents and anxiously awaited the return of her husband and her parents-in-law to Seoul after it was recaptured by the United Nations and the South Korean forces. Most of the Seoulites who had left eventually returned, but her husband and his family did not. In the meantime, she had realized that she was pregnant. On February 2, 1951, before Seoul was recaptured by the south, she gave birth to a daughter in the home of her parents. She knew, however, that her newborn daughter could not be registered as the legitimate child of Ch'ang-su and herself because they had not yet registered their marriage in the township registration office. Their marriage was not legal. Consequently, her daughter, Hae-suk, could not use Ch'ang-su's surname. Instead, Ok-ja's family name was given as her last name, which was exceptional in Korean custom.

The failure to record a marriage right after the ceremony is not unusual. Many married couples often delay this requirement until a convenient time arises. Almost every Korean has two marriage dates, the actual date and the legally recorded one. For example, I was married on June 25, but I didn't register my marriage until October 29. In extreme cases a marriage may not be legally registered for years.[2] This same practice is also observed in Japan.[3]

Ok-ja stayed with her parents until the middle of March 1951. Knowing that she could not depend on her parents for her support, she took menial jobs, moving from one place to another throughout the south with her infant daughter. Finally they settled in Wŏnju. Hae-suk finished high school there and got a job at a post office as a telephone operator. Ok-ja went to live with her daughter when Hae-suk married a man who worked in a pharmaceutical company. Ok-ja spent most of her time taking care of her grandchildren.

Ch'ang-su had followed the United States Army arsenal to its new location in Pusan. His sister, Kyŏng-suk, with their parents, had also ended up in Pusan. She searched the military arsenals and finally found Ch'ang-su. He was deeply disappointed to learn that Ok-ja was not with his family. Later, he changed jobs to work for a relief organization under United Nations sponsorship. He and his family stayed in Pusan until 1955.

Ch'ang-su claimed that he had been unable to obtain the pass that was required to cross the Han River to Seoul and also that later he was unable to take time off from his job to search for his wife. It is difficult to believe that he made a serious effort to find his separated wife. Had he tried sooner to come back to Seoul, he would at least have had a chance to find her and their newborn daughter while they were still at Ok-ja's natal home.

He was naive, if not negligent. When he returned to Seoul in the spring of 1955, and went to his wife's natal home, the family had moved, and no one seemed to know where the family had relocated.

In 1960, not having found his wife, Ch'ang-su remarried. His second wife was a widow who had four children, all girls, from her previous marriage. Although in reality this was a second marriage for Ch'ang-su, legally he was an eligible bachelor because his previous marriage to Ok-ja had not been registered. This time, he registered his marriage promptly.

The new wife brought one of her daughters to live with her and Ch'ang-su and the other three daughters maintained a separate residence. Ch'ang-su had to support his own household, which included his elderly mother, and that of his three step-daughters. Under the increasing tension and financial burden, the couple encountered all kinds of problems. In the mid-1970s Ch'ang-su divorced his second wife. At the time he was reunited with his first wife and daughter, he was living with his aged mother and renting out rooms in their home. The reunion of Ch'ang-su and Ok-ja was not initiated by either one of them. It resulted from the efforts of their daughter, Hae-suk. As did tens of thousands of other people, Hae-suk watched the reunion telethon carefully, hoping that her father might be seeking her and her mother. She said later: "Once the reunion telethon started, all I did was watch the television. I didn't even sleep. I was also trying to observe how my mother was reacting. She seemed calm and didn't display any particular emotion about the telethon. I was sure though that she was anxious to know what had happened to my father. She didn't say anything about it, but she kept on watching the television just like I did."

On the first night of the reunion telethon there was an announcement that the national police headquarters computer could be used to search for missing family members. Hae-suk decided that she wanted to seek her father. She wrote down the address and telephone number of the office of the computer center of the national police headquarters. Hae-suk asked her mother about her idea, but Ok-ja did not express any sentiment one way or another. Hae-suk interpreted her mother's neutral response as approval. "But," she said, "my mother and I thought that if he were alive, he had probably remarried. We were worried that if we went on the telethon looking for him we might harm his life with his new family."

On the night she began thinking about looking for her father, Hae-suk had a dream in which a dark-suited man told her that he was her father. Hae-suk said, "I guess I dreamed about him because I was thinking about him a lot and talking about him all the time. When I told my mother

about the dream, she said 'Yesterday was your father's sixtieth birthday.'"
A person's sixtieth birthday in Korea is still a commemorated occasion.
The average life span of an individual used to be a lot shorter than it is
now, and reaching sixty years of age was a significant accomplishment. In
addition, "according to the traditional system of time reckoning prevalent
throughout East Asia, 60 years is the length of one complete cycle. Thus,
a parent's sixtieth birthday is marked by a major celebration, traditionally
held to denote the completion of an active life."[4]

Hae-suk interpreted her mother's acknowledgment of her father's sixtieth birthday as another positive sign encouraging her to search. She went
to Seoul immediately and filed an application at the national police headquarters. She chose the computer matching system over the reunion telethon to avoid publicly disrupting the family life of her father if he should
have remarried. Hae-suk begged the officer to conduct the search without notifying her father or his family, but the officer told her that some
verification by the person sought would be required. Because even the
computer search would become known to her father and his family if he
were located, Hae-suk decided to register with KBS also. Realizing that
her turn to appear on the telethon would be many days away, she returned
home. Hae-suk avoided talking about her father to her mother, and for
nearly two weeks nothing happened.

On July 20 the police station near her home notified Hae-suk to contact the computer center of the police headquarters, an indication that the
computer had finally identified Hae-suk's father, Ch'ang-su Han. Hae-suk
called the center immediately. The center monitored a phone conversation
between Hae-suk and her father, but the reception linking several phones
was so poor that she could not understand much, other than the persistent inquiry as to whether her mother had remarried. She told Ch'ang-su
that her mother had not. They ended their call by agreeing to meet at the
center the next day with Ok-ja accompanying Hae-suk.

Hae-suk was not satisfied with the brief conversation. She could not
wait until the next day without knowing whether her father was remarried
and had a new family. But she did not want to make another call in her
mother's presence, considering her emotional state, so she went to her
husband's office to call the center and ascertain her father's marital status.
When she was told by the officer at the center that Ch'ang-su was single, she could hardly control her emotions. She returned home to tell her
mother. Ok-ja tried to be calm, but was obviously affected by the news.

The journey of Ok-ja and her daughter Hae-suk to Seoul the next day to be reunited with the husband and father from whom they had been separated for thirty-two long years was emotional. In the computer center at noon the two anxious women saw an aged man enter in front of the swarm of reporters and cameramen. As soon as Ch'ang-su saw Ok-ja, he told an officer, "That's her!" Ok-ja also recognized him immediately. Ok-ja told her daughter, "That's your father." Hae-suk rushed toward him, shouting "Father! Father!" Ch'ang-su hugged her and put one of his arms around the shoulder of his wife Ok-ja. They could not talk at all for a while. The three of them cried for a long period. After a brief interview with the reporters, they went to Ch'ang-su's house to see his elderly mother. Hae-suk's grandmother wept while holding the hands of her granddaughter, whom she had never seen before.

Three days later Ch'ang-su went to Hae-suk's home in Wŏnju to spend several days with Ok-ja. Ch'ang-su and Ok-ja agreed to live together, forming a family again. Ch'ang-su started the long process of correcting the official family records, which involved many legal entanglements. Hae-suk's surname needed to be changed to Han from Park. Hae-suk was quite happy and only regretted that there was no male heir in her natal family.

Ok-ja said: "We spent several days together, but we really didn't have much to talk about. He wanted to explain what had happened to him after Seoul was recaptured, but I did not want to know any more about it. That's all in the past now." Ok-ja had apparently forgiven Ch'ang-su. Instead, she was worrying about their future: "He doesn't have any savings or even a steady job. And we also have to take care of his mother. But I don't think I can live off my daughter any longer, particularly now that I'm with my husband. I don't know what to do."

This fulfilling reunion did not solve all the family's problems. Instead, it brought about a different problem—finding a means of livelihood for the reunited couple, who have suddenly acquired new responsibilities and burdens.

CHAPTER 9
Faithful Endurance

FAITHFUL ENDURANCE

In the fall of 1978 Larry T. McGehee, an educator, a syndicated columnist for southern newspapers, and a good friend of mine, wrote a sentimental column, thinking of a daughter who was away from home for college. He wrote:

Last Saturday we took our eldest off to college. . . . it seems to us she is somewhere off in another century and on the other side of the globe. . . . We thought we were immune from the anxieties and blues we have seen September after September on the college campuses we've served or attended for 25 years now, where other parents have delivered their offspring up tearfully and nervously into the hands of strangers. When our turn came, we knew, we would go cheerfully and stoically. But ever since we drove away, there's been a chill in the evening air. . . . Her mother vacuums her room a lot more than it is accustomed to. . . . We eat a lot of pizza with pepperoni, as if the taste will bring her home.

. . . How is it for the very first time, 30 years after it really happened, we suddenly feel we have actually left our parents' homes, just because our daughter has just left ours? . . . And four nights later, it's 10:28 in the evening, and I wonder if she's waiting until the rates change at 11:00 to call. A few minutes ago the television flashed its nightly question: "It's ten o'clock. Do you know where your children are?" We do know. Far too well.[1]

McGehee is an astute writer and has a knack for literary expression. Even those who cannot describe things as he does, however, can share his sentiments. Ever since I have sent off my oldest child to college, from this flat land of Tennessee to the hills of Amherst, I cannot keep my monthly phone bill down. If sending children away from home for college or marriage affects parents so strongly, what must be the agony of people who are more or less permanently separated from their family members? And who are separated without any way of communicating with one another? No one can adequately describe the poignant anguish of dispersed families.

There are no indications when the sundered families of Korea, particularly those divided by the DMZ, will have a chance to be reunited. As described earlier, from September 20 to 23, 1985, 50 well-selected individuals from dispersed families from each side of divided Korea, along with 101 entertainers and support personnel, visited the capital city of the opposing regime. More than half of the dispersed people from each side were reunited with other family members, although the reunions were brief. This was a dramatic event in the history of the Korean partition, but no additional progress has been made since it occurred.

No one knows when Korean reunification might be achieved, although political rhetoric on the subject flourishes. Young Whan Khil, a political scientist who is knowledgeble about both Koreas, pessimistically stated: "From my visit to North Korea I came away with the impression that the issue of Korean unification would be indeed difficult to resolve. The problem may not be settled in the lifetime of that generation of Koreans who experienced liberation in 1945 and went through the Korean War in 1950–1953. . . . my intellect and my instinct as a hard-nosed realist tell me that the situation in the Korean peninsula is hopelessly stalemated."[2]

A fundamental distrust between North and South Korea still persists. Manwoo Lee, who visited both Koreas, wrote: "If I learned anything from the trip in the summer of 1981, it is that neither side wants another war. In P'yŏngyang I told my hosts that the U.S. troops and the South Korean armed forces are not offensive but defensive. They did not believe me. In Seoul I told some responsible people that P'yŏngyang is not interested in attacking Seoul and that P'yŏngyang is very defensive. They did not believe me. . . . So far, both sides have mobilized their best brains to misread each other."[3]

In the minds of all Koreans the issue of family reunification cannot be separated from the agenda for national reunification. As the history of Korea astonishingly reveals, in spite of foreign invasions and colonization by its much larger and stronger neighbors, that is, China, Russia, and Japan, Korea has maintained its identity and continuity. According to Gregory Henderson, its "smallness of dimension, stability of boundaries, ethnic and religious homogeneity, and *exceptional historical continuity marks Korea* [emphasis mine]."[4] Considering this, I am optimistic that the issue of Korean national reunification is not a matter of "if" but of "when." In a five-thousand-year history, forty years of political disunity may not seem long, but to the millions of dispersed families they have seemed like an eternity of faithful endurance.

NATIVE VOICES

In this study I have tried to understand the situations of the participants from their perspectives. I hope that to a certain extent I have been successful in doing so because of my position as a native, an insider, and a victim of the war.

I was startled to discover the paucity of written work on the subject of dispersed families in the Korean mass media. This was partially due to political sensitivity as I have indicated elsewhere. In fact, up until 1973, suggestions, comments, or inducements regarding the reunion of dispersed family members in the north and the south were taboo and subject to governmental censorship. In 1971, when Man-sup Lee, a leading congressman of the ruling party and a trusted friend of the president of South Korea, wrote a book of essays to foster a reunion movement among sundered families, an ex-director of the KCIA, Hyŏng-uk Kim, and an ex-minister of justice, Pok-ki Min, accused Lee of violating the anticommunist law.

Thus, it is understandable why most South Korean writers have been reluctant to express their views on this subject. They have been fully aware of the possible repercussions. Only if they have politically supported the government have many intellectuals, scholars, writers, or journalists been willing to give their opinions. In the winter of 1984, after completing a draft of this book, I was surprised to learn in checking with my informants that some of them were concerned about how I had described the incident of my aunt's death. I had stated that "it was not the bullet of the enemy but that of the United Nations and South Korean air forces," that had killed her. Apparently I was not supposed to say such a thing, even if it was true.

I tried to understand native voices by reading Korean fiction. I collected dozens of well-received novels written about family dispersal and the partition of the nation[5] and read them all, but I was unable to grasp any pattern. As many critics have pointed out, these novels have avoided coming to grips with fundamental human issues, free from politics.[6] Most of the writers have tended to be fatalistic about the dispersed families,[7] and uncritical of the political status quo. Their euphemism for dispersal is *han,* a Korean word meaning "unrequited resentment" (adapting the translation of Laurel Kendall).[8] Thus are possible political censorship and censure avoided.

Since the reunion telethon and its vivid portrayal of human tragedy, however, some Korean writers have begun to rethink their work.[9] Perhaps in the future native voices will be free from restraint.

THE EMOTIONAL BURDEN OF FIELDWORK

For the first time as an anthropologist, I totally immersed myself in the field situation and in the people I was studying. During the reunion telethon, I spent many nights weeping along with the participants as I heard the tragic stories of separation and witnessed the joy and emotion of the reunions. Portions of my field notes were stained with my tears.

In my previous fieldwork in other cultures, after I had returned from the field, I soon got over certain emotional moments I had experienced. I could talk about them as freely as if they had happened to someone else. During this project, however, and even after my return to my university, I did not want to talk about my field experiences with others. Even now that two years have passed since my last trip to Korea in the winter of 1984, I cannot escape my emotional involvement.[10] Had I not developed a compassionate attachment to the people I studied, however, I do not think I could consider myself a decent human being. Being an "objective" scientist does not mean that one has to be uninvolved or impersonal.

Another aspect of my involvement in this study is my own history. My life story cannot be told without telling the story of war and death. When I was born, Korea was still occupied by the Japanese, and my family and I lived under colonial rule. During World War II, when I was five years old, my eldest brother was drafted into the Japanese imperial army and was sent to the battlefield somewhere in China. (He later escaped and joined the army of the Korean independence movement K'wangbokun, sponsored by the Korean provisional government in Shanghai. This army fought with the Chinese army against the Japanese. My brother came back to Korea in 1946 when the provisional government returned after the war.) I remember having to seek shelter when American B-29 planes flew over. When I was six years old and a first grader in elementary school, I was expelled for refusing to collect brass bowls and chopsticks to make artillery shells for the Japanese imperial army.

After World War II the chaos of postwar Korean society threatened the safety of many Koreans, as ideological struggles led Koreans to fight one another. My hometown, located in mountainous northeastern Kyŏngsang Puk-do in South Korea, was controlled by the south in the daytime but became the colony of communist guerrillas at night. The oscillation of these two political powers between day and night resulted in the deaths of many innocent villagers. The fratricidal Korean War broke out when I was in the sixth grade (I had been able to return to school after the end of World War II).

When I went to Korea during my study, one of my cousins (my mother's sister's son) always came to the airport to pick me up. As I shook his hand, I could not help but notice the scar on his hand, caused by a machine-gun bullet fired from an airplane during the Korean War. The same bullet had killed his mother (my aunt) instantly. As they were fleeing from Seoul, they had been outdistanced by the fast-retreating South Korean army and had gotten trapped behind the enemy's defense line during an air raid. My project also unintentionally brought back sad memories for my wife, because her mother was killed during the Korean War. I still have such profound and dreadful memories of air raids and bombings that whenever I hear the sound of jet airplanes, I recall the horror of that war.

It has been difficult for me to write about myself and "my own people" and yet remain objective. In this book I have tried to maintain a balance between the "compassion" of being a native anthropologist doing field-work with "my own people" and the "detachment" of being a "scientist." In attempting to depict the struggles of millions of sundered Koreans, the anguish of the war that I also experienced tortured me day after day. It was painful to complete this book. Nonetheless, as Miles Richardson once asked, "If the anthropologist does not tell the human myth, then who will?"[11]

Notes

Preface

1. Although my work does not include extracting strict contrast sets, formal componential analysis, or the other usual appurtenances, it can be considered within the *emic* approach of ethnoscience. See Ward Goodenough, "Componential Analysis and The Study of Meaning," *Language*, 32 (1956): 195–216; and William C. Sturtevant, "Studies in Ethnoscience," *American Anthropologist*, 66, pt. 2 (1964): 99–131.

2. See Francis L. K. Hsu, "The Effect of Dominant Kinship Relationships on Kin and Non-Kin Behavior: A Hypothesis," *American Anthropologist*, 67 (1965): 638–661; idem, ed., *Kinship and Culture* (Chicago: Aldine Publishing Co., 1971); and idem, *Rugged Individualism Reconsidered: Essays in Psychological Anthropology* (Knoxville: University of Tennessee Press, 1983).

Chapter 1. Korean Family Dispersal

1. Bruce Cumings recounts well the genesis of the Korean War. See Bruce Cumings, *The Origins of the Korean War: Liberation and the Emergence of Separate Regimes 1945–1947* (Princeton: Princeton University Press, 1981).

2. Harry J. Middleton, *The Compact History of the Korean War* (New York: Hawthorn Books, 1965), 230.

3. Republic of Korea National Red Cross, *The Dispersed Families in Korea* (Seoul: Republic of Korea National Red Cross, 1977), 71.

4. "The U.N. estimated military casualties at between one and a half and two million, and North Korean civilian casualties at one million" (Middleton, *The Compact History*, 230).

5.   According to a recent nationwide survey by the *Hankook Ilbo* newspaper on the awareness of Koreans toward the Korean War, the majority of the respondents (76 percent) did not have firsthand experience with the war; of these, 41.1 percent indicated that they had learned about the war from school textbooks and 29.5 percent from other sources such as novels and other documents. By and large, the respondents admitted that they were unaware of the misery of the war. Amazingly, 80.4 percent of the respondents who belonged to the 18 to 24 age group said they knew little about the war. (See *Hankook Ilbo*, June 27, 1984).

6.   Miles Richardson, "Anthropologist—The Myth Teller," *American Ethnologist*, 2 (1975): 520.

7.   See Choong Soon Kim, *An Asian Anthropologist in the South: Field Experiences with Blacks, Indians, and Whites* (Knoxville: University of Tennessee Press, 1977).

8.   John H. Peterson, Jr., Barbara G. Spencer, and Choong S. Kim, *Choctaw Demographic Survey* (Philadelphia, Miss.: Mississippi Band of Choctaw Indians, 1974).

9.   James W. Fernandez, "Reflections on Looking into Mirrors," *Semiotica*, 30 (1980): 36.

10.   See Emiko Ohnuki-Tierney, *Illness and Culture in Contemporary Japan: An Anthropological View* (New York: Cambridge University Press, 1984), 1–18; idem, " 'Native' Anthropologists," *American Ethnologist*, 11 (1984): 584–586; Barbara G. Myerhoff, *Number Our Days* (New York: Simon and Schuster, 1980); and Barbara G. Myerhoff and Jay Ruby, "Introduction," in *A Crack in the Mirror*, edited by Jay Ruby (Philadelphia: University of Pennsylvania Press, 1982), 1–35.

11.   Some probability-sample-minded (or quantitative-method-oriented) social scientists might raise a reasonable question. Simeon W. Chilungu once blasted the work of Monica Wilson: "In *Good Company*, for example, Wilson (1951) reports that she and her husband collected information about the Nyakusa, who totalled approximately 234,000, from four key informants" (Simeon W. Chilungu, "Issues in the Ethics of Research Method: An Interpretation of the Anglo-American Perspective," *Current Anthropology*, 17 [1976]: 460). See also Monica Wilson, *Good Company: A Study of Nyakusa Agevillages* (London: Oxford University Press, 1951).

12.   L. L. Langness defines the life history method as "an extensive record of a person's life as it is reported either by the person himself or by others or both, and whether it is written or in interviews or both" (L. L. Langness, *The Life History in Anthropological Science* [New York: Holt, Rinehart and Winston, 1965], 4–5).

13.   I attempted to take this tour in the summer of 1981, but I had not allowed sufficient time for the Korean authorities to check my records. In the summer of 1982 I submitted my application well in advance of the tour.

14.   Roger Rosenblatt describes vividly the disquieting and ennobling portraits of the children growing up in the war zones of the world. See Roger Rosenblatt, *Children of War* (Garden City: Anchor Books, 1983).

15.   John L. Gwaltney and Joseph Aceves have also used relatives and friends as key informants in their fieldwork. See John L. Gwaltney, "Common Sense and Science: Urban Core Black Observations," in *Anthropologists at Home in North America: Methods and Issues in the Study of One's Own Society*, edited by Donald A. Messer-

schmidt (New York: Cambridge University Press, 1981), 49; Joseph Aceves, *Social Change in a Spanish Village* (Cambridge, Mass.: Schenkman Publishing Co., 1971), 4–5; and Joseph Aceves, "Competence by Blood: Ethnological Fieldwork in the Ancestral Village" (Paper presented at the seventy-seventh annual meeting of the American Anthropological Association, Los Angeles, November 14–18, 1978).

16. "In general informants seem most likely to give deceptive information in three situations: (1) when information is sought from which a person's failure in role performance can be inferred, (2) when information is sought which might reveal deviations from valued cultural norms, and (3) when the information sought is a marker of social rank" (Clark W. Sorensen, "Patterns of Misinformation in South Korean Fieldwork" [Paper presented at the eighty-fourth annual meeting of the American Anthropological Association, Washington, D.C., December 4–8, 1985]).

17. Aceves used a similar technique of having several reliable informants as a review panel for his ideas. See Aceves, *Social Change*, 7.

18. In fact, "some life histories of considerable anthropological importance have been collected by individuals who were not themselves anthropologists" (Pertti J. Pelto, *Anthropological Research: The Structure of Inquiry* [New York: Harper and Row, 1970], 99). The narrative of John Tanner by Edwin James is well known to anthropologists who are interested in this method. See Edwin James, *The Thirty Years of Indian Captivity of John Tanner* (Minneapolis: Ross and Haines, 1956).

19. Margaret Park Redfield, ed., *Human Nature and The Study of Society: The Papers of Robert Redfield*, vol. 1 (Chicago: University of Chicago Press, 1962), vi.

20. Ibid., 67.

21. See William Graham Sumner, *Folkways* (New York: New American Library, 1959); Alexis de Tocqueville, *Democracy in America*, translated by Henry Reeve, 2 vols. (New York: Co-operative Publication Society, 1900); and Thorstein Veblen, *The Theory of the Leisure Class* (New York: Modern Library, 1934).

22. Redfield, *Human Nature*, 61, 63.

23. James W. Fernandez, *Bwiti: An Ethnography of the Religious Imagination in Africa* (Princeton: Princeton University Press, 1982), xx.

24. Ibid.

25. Anthony F. C. Wallace made an analogy between "slash-and-burn agriculture" and theory-building in cultural anthropology: "After cultivating a field for a while, the natives move on to a new one and let the bush take over; then they return, slash and burn and raise crops in the old field again" (Anthony F. C. Wallace, "Review of: *The Revolution in Anthropology* by I. C. Jarvie," *American Anthropologist*, 68 [1966]: 1254). A successive transition occurs even in a mature science such as physics in accordance with Thomas S. Kuhn. See Thomas S. Kuhn, *The Structure of Scientific Revolutions* (Chicago: University of Chicago Press, 1962), 12.

26. Donald A. Messerschmidt listed five reasons for this trend. See Donald A. Messerschmidt, "On Anthropology at Home," in *Anthropologists at Home in North America: Methods and Issues in the Study of One's Own Society*, edited by Donald A. Messerschmidt (New York: Cambridge University Press, 1981), 9–13.

27. Ibid., 13.

28.   G. K. Nukunya, *Kinship and Marriage among the Anlo Ewe* (New York: Humanities Press, 1969), 18–19.

29.   Choong Soon Kim, *An Asian Anthropologist*, 15.

30.   Hortense Powdermaker, *Stranger and Friend: The Way of an Anthropologist* (New York: W. W. Norton, 1966), 13.

31.   See Myrna Sayles, "Behind Locked Doors," in *Applied Anthropology in America*, edited by Elizabeth Eddy and William L. Partridge (New York: Columbia University Press, 1978), 201–228.

32.   John L. Aguilar, "Inside Research: An Ethnography of a Debate," in *Anthropologists at Home in North America: Methods and Issues in the Study of One's Own Society*, edited by Donald A. Messerschmidt (New York: Cambridge University Press, 1981), 15.

33.   See Aceves, *Social Change*, v; and Myerhoff and Ruby, "Introduction," 33.

34.   Ohnuki-Tierney, *Illness and Culture*, 13; M. N. Srinivas, *Social Change in Modern India* (Berkeley: University of California Press, 1966), 157; and M. Dalton, *Men Who Manage* (New York: Wiley, 1959), 283.

35.   Emiko Ohnuki-Tierney, *Illness and Healing among the Sakhalin Ainu: A Symbolic Interpretation* (New York: Cambridge University Press, 1981); idem, *Illness and Culture*, 1–18; and idem, " 'Native' Anthropologists," 584–586.

36.   Fernandez, "Reflections," 36.

37.   Ohnuki-Tierney, *Illness and Culture*, 12–13.

38.   Srinivas, *Social Change*, 155. And some anthropologists believe that experience in an alien culture is a prerequisite for studying one's own culture. See Clyde Kluckhohn, *Mirror for Man: The Relation of Anthropology to Modern Life* (New York: McGraw-Hill, 1949), 9; and George D. Spindler, "An Anthropology of Education," *Council on Anthropology and Education Newsletter*, 4 (1973): 14–16.

39.   Donald A. Messerschmidt, ed., *Anthropologists at Home in North America: Methods and Issues in the Study of One's Own Society* (New York: Cambridge University Press, 1981), 273.

40.   Lawrence Hennigh, "The Anthropologist as Key Informant: Inside a Rural Oregon Town," in *Anthropologists at Home in North America: Methods and Issues in the Study of One's Own Society*, edited by Donald A. Messerschmidt (New York: Cambridge University Press, 1981), 121–132.

41.   Srinivas, *Social Change*, 154.

42.   See the "Principles of Professional Responsibility" adopted by the Council of the American Anthropological Association, May 1971. See also Michael A. Rynkiewich and James P. Spradley, eds., *Ethics and Anthropology: Dilemmas in Fieldwork* (New York: John Wiley and Sons, 1976); in a special issue on the ethical problems of fieldwork, Joan Cassell and Murray L. Wax, eds., "Ethical Problems of Fieldwork," *Social Problems*, 27 (1980): 259–370; and George L. Hicks, "Informant Anonymity and Scientific Accuracy: The Problem of Pseudonyms," *Human Organization*, 36 (1977): 214–220.

43.   The South Korean anthropologist Mun Woong Lee published a book on North Korea in English; it was based primarily on secondary sources and not on his fieldwork in the north. See Mun Woong Lee, *Rural North Korea under Communism: A Study of Socioeconomic Change* (Houston: Rice University Press,

1976); and idem, "Kongsan ch'aejae ha'ae sŏŭi ch'injok chojik: Ibuk ŭi kyŏngu (Kinship organization under communism: A North Korean case study), *"Han'guk munhwa illyuhak* (Korean cultural anthropology), 9 (1977): 127–129.

Chapter 2. Historical Background

1. Shannon McCune, *Korea: The Land of Broken Calm* (New York: D. Van Nostrand, 1966).
2. Sui forces attacked Korea in 598 and in 612. See Woo-keun Han, *The History of Korea* (Seoul: Eul-yoo Publishing Co., 1981), 26. During the military invasions by the T'ang dynasty of China in the seventh century, many Korean captives from Paekche and Koguryŏ were taken to and relocated throughout China as slaves. See Kyoo-whan Hyun, *Han'guk iyumin-sa* (A history of Korean wanderers and emigrants), 2 vols. (Seoul: Ŏmunkak, 1967), 1: 50–51. In 1636 the Manchu state of the Late Ch'ing invaded Yi Korea. Again, large numbers of Koreans became captives and were taken to Manchuria.
3. During the medieval period of the Koryŏ dynasty (918–1392), scores of people were captured by the Khitans and were taken to Khitan territory. One Khitan province, for instance, included nearly five thousand people from Koryŏ, composing their own province (Kyoo-whan Hyun, *Han'guk iyumin-sa*, 1: 55). The most devastating family dispersals occurred during the Mongol invasions of the Koryŏ reign in 1253, 1257, and 1273. During the rule of King Kojong (1213–1259) of Koryŏ, 206,000 Koryŏ civilians were captured by the Mongols (ibid., 57–60). After the invasion the Mongols not only instituted royal marriages but also required human tribute, particularly unmarried females, from Koryŏ. Most of those women who were taken to Peking became concubines or slaves of the Yuan emperor and of Mongol aristocrats (ibid., 68).
4. Japanese pirates during the thirteenth and fourteenth centuries captured some four thousand Koreans and took them to Japan as prisoners. See Kyoo-whan Hyun, *Han'guk iyumin-sa*, 2: 273–291; Edward W. Wagner, *The Korean Minority in Japan: 1904–1950* (New York: Institute of Pacific Relations, 1951), 6; and Yoshi S. Kuno, *Japanese Expression on the Asiatic Continent*, 2 vols. (Berkeley: University of California Press, 1937), 1: 176). Although the Japanese pirates were troublesome, the Japanese attacks on Korea from 1590–1597, under the leadership of Toyotomi Hideyoshi, were devastating. Hideyoshi's forces invaded Korea, resulting in a massive number of casualties and captives. The occupational list of those taken captive included highly skilled workmen and artisans such as weavers, porcelain manufacturers, and priests. They even captured Confucian scholars. See Abe Yoshio, *Nihon shushigaku to Chōsen* (Japanese Neo-Confucianism and Korea) (Tokyo: Tokyo University Press, 1965); idem, "Nihon jukyō no hatten to Yi T'oegye (The development of Confucianism in Japan and Yi T'oegye)," *Han*, 1 (1972): 3–27; Changsoo Lee and George DeVos, *Koreans in Japan: Ethnic Conflict and Accommodation* (Berkeley: University of California Press, 1981), 14; Mary Elizabeth Berry, *Hideyoshi* (Cambridge: Harvard University Press, 1982).
5. Gregory Henderson, *Korea: The Politics of the Vortex* (Cambridge: Harvard University Press, 1968), 13.

6. Kyoo-whan Hyun, *Han'guk iyumin-sa*, 1: 173.

7. Ibid., 2: 425.

8. According to a survey made by the office of the governor-general in Korea in 1931, based on a sample of 201 Korean families in Manchuria, the great majority had moved to Manchuria for economic reasons (96.1 percent). Only 3.4 percent had moved for political reasons, and the rest (0.5 percent) had moved for other reasons, such as the result of travel or on the advice of relatives (source: *Manchuria and Koreans*, Governor-General of Japan in Korea, 1931). Because the survey was conducted and analyzed by the Japanese colonial government, some Koreans might not have given honest answers for fear of possible repercussions from the Japanese authorities.

9. Kyoo-whan Hyun, *Han'guk iyumin-sa*, 1: 648. Cf. Chae-Jin Lee, *China's Korean Minority: The Politics of Ethnic Education* (Boulder: Westview Press, 1986), 20.

10. Kyoo-whan Hyun, *Han'guk iyumin-sa*, 1: 648–649.

11. According to the office of the census of the People's Republic of China, by July 1982 the Korean population in China was 1,763,870. See Lee, *China's Korean Minority*, 2–3; and Ung [Peter] Hyun and Pong-hak Hyun, *Chung-gong ŭi han'in tŭl* (Koreans in the People's Republic of China) (Seoul: Pomyang-sa, 1984), 11.

12. About 4,600 Koreans in Manchuria joined the Chinese forces in fighting against their southern brethren. See Chae-Jin Lee, *China's Korean Minority*, 62; see also the detailed accounts of Yong-whan Ch'a in Kyoo-whan Hyun, *Han'guk iyumin-sa*, 1: 657.

13. See Chae-Jin Lee, *China's Korean Minority*, 68, 163; see also a series of special reports on Koreans in Manchuria in *The Korea Times Chicago Edition*, September 7, 9, 10, 1983.

14. Xiatong Fei, "Toward a People's Anthropology," *Human Organization*, 39 (1980): 119; Lee, *China's Korean Minority*, 77–95. Fei has been president of the Chinese Sociological Association and deputy director and professor at the Institute of Nationality Studies of the Chinese Academy of Social Sciences in Beijing.

15. Chae-Jin Lee, *China's Korean Minority*, 66–67, 152; *The Korea Times Chicago Edition*, April 2, 1984.

16. See "Travelog of Pong-hak Hyun," in *The Korea Times Chicago Edition*, August 3, 4, 10, 18, 1983.

17. *Hankook Ilbo*, March 29, 30, 1984.

18. *The Korea Times Chicago Edition*, September 7, 9, 10, 1983.

19. Articles by the special assignment reporters of *The Korea Times Chicago Edition*, September 7, 9, 10, 1983.

20. *Hankook Ilbo*, March 28, 1984.

21. Ibid., March 29, 30, 1984; see also Chae-Jin Lee, *China's Korean Minority*, 146–147.

22. Exceptionally, in January 1965 an elderly couple, Yong-whan Ch'a and his wife, returned to South Korea for a reunion with their son. In December 1978 Han-bin Ahn, a doctor of herbal medicine, and his wife returned to South Korea permanently via Hong Kong.

23. *Dong-A Ilbo*, May 12, 1979.

24. *Joong-ang Ilbo*, October 26, 1976.

25. *Hankook Ilbo*, March 28, 1984.

26. *Joong-ang Ilbo*, March 28, 1984.

27. *Korea Newsreview*, March 31, 1984.

28. Ibid.

29. *The Korea Times English Section*, March 27, 1984.

30. *Korea Newsreview*, March 5, 1984.

31. Archaeological evidence is in Edward Kidder, *Prehistoric Japanese Arts: Jomon Pottery* (Palo Alto: Kodansha International, 1968), 75; Gari Ledyard, "Galloping along with the Horseriders: Looking for the Founders of Japan," *Journal of Japanese Studies*, 2 (1976): 217–254; Kyoo-whan Hyun, *Han'guk iyumin-sa*, 2: 11–44; and Changsoo Lee and DeVos, *Koreans in Japan*, 3–13. Linguistic evidence is discussed in Harumi Befu, *Japan: An Anthropological Introduction* (New York: Thomas Y. Crowell, 1971), 17.

32. Ironically, as the Korean population in Japan increased, the Japanese population in Korea also increased. See Changsoo Lee and DeVos, *Koreans in Japan*, 34. By 1940 nearly 700,000 Japanese were in Korea. See Andrew J. Grajdanzev, *Modern Korea* (New York: Octagon Books, 1978), 75–79; and Irene Tauber, *The Population of Japan* (Princeton: Princeton University Press, 1958), 188.

33. See Republic of Korea National Red Cross, *The Dispersed Families*, 40.

34. Ibid.

35. Changsoo Lee and DeVos, *Koreans in Japan*, 53.

36. Republic of Korea National Red Cross, *The Dispersed Families*, 42.

37. William J. Gane, *Repatriation: From 25 September 1945 to 31 December 1945* (Seoul: U.S. Military Government in Korea, 1947), 14.

38. An interview with Yoshida Seiji, MBC-TV (South Korea), June 3, 1984. See the transcript of the interview with Yoshida, who was in charge of drafting Koreans in Kyŏngsang, Chŏlla, and Cheju provinces, by Sun-t'ae Mun, *Yosong Dong-A*, 246 (June 1984): 393–397.

39. Changsoo Lee and DeVos, *Koreans in Japan*, 60.

40. Ibid., 106–107.

41. According to a survey conducted in 1954, 96.6 percent of Korean residents in Japan were from South Korea, and only 2.4 percent were from North Korea. See Changsoo Lee and DeVos, *Koreans in Japan*, 104.

42. Sung Chul Yang, *Korea and Two Regimes: Kim Il Sung and Park Chung Hee* (Cambridge, Mass.: Schenkman Publishing Co., 1981), 252–256.

43. Changsoo Lee and DeVos, *Koreans in Japan*, 151.

44. According to Befu, regarding Japanese views on foreigners, "Orientals, particularly Koreans, are accorded a lower status than Japanese" (Befu, *Japan*, 125). Also, in a survey on June 20, 1983, by the Japanese government, which included a random sample of three thousand Japanese, the majority of the respondents (51 percent) said that they felt unfriendly toward Korea and Koreans. See *Hankook Ilbo*, April 23, 1984.

45. For more details, see Kyŏng-sik Pak, *Chōsenjin kyoseirenkō no kiroku* (A record of involuntary Korean migration) (Tokyo: Miraisha, 1965); Wagner, *The Korean Minority in Japan*; Richard H. Mitchell, *The Korean Minority in Japan*

(Berkeley: University of California Press, 1967); and Changsoo Lee and DeVos, *Koreans in Japan*.

46. Kyoo-whan Hyun, *Han'guk iyumin-sa*, 1: 786–963.

47. Ibid.

48. Kyoo-whan Hyun, *Han'guk iyumin-sa*, 2: 751.

49. *Joong-ang Ilbo*, September 6, 1982.

50. According to Hyun's report in 1967, of the 43,000 Koreans on Sakhalin 65 percent obtained North Korean citizenship, 25 percent chose Russian citizenship, and 10 percent remained denationalized inhabitants. See Kyoo-whan Hyun, *Han'guk iyumin-sa*, 2: 751–752.

51. *Dong-A Ilbo*, June 6, 1973.

52. During the Japanese repatriation in 1957, however, approximately 2,300 Koreans who married Japanese women managed to be included in the repatriation package. Some Koreans on the island married Japanese women simply to take advantage of the repatriation opportunity. There were some instances of a so-called term contract for marriage, wherein marriages would be terminated upon repatriation to Japan. See *Joong-ang Ilbo*, July 5, 1982; see also Republic of Korea National Red Cross, *The Dispersed Families*, 123.

53. *Dong-A Ilbo*, June 4, 1983.

54. Kyoo-whan Hyun, *Han'guk iyumin-sa*, 2: 751–752.

55. Its formal name was the Korean Mission in Japan, because the normalization treaty between the two countries was not signed, and neither country recognized the other.

56. Kyoo-whan Hyun, *Han'guk iyumin-sa*, 2: 758.

57. When the Soviets relaxed the conditions for exit visas from 1962 to 1976, Japan was reluctant to issue entry visas. When Japan was agreeable to issuing entry visas, in 1975 for instance, the Soviets refused to issue exit visas. South Korea has insisted that the Japanese government should facilitate them by granting the same legal status as that of other Korean residents in Japan. Japan has maintained its position that the Japanese government would willingly negotiate with the Russian authorities if the final destination of Koreans in Sakhalin is South Korea. The position of the Soviets seems to be hedged by objections of North Korea against Soviet patronage in the repatriation process of Koreans in Sakhalin to South Korea.

58. See Roy E. Appleman, *United States Army in the Korean War: South to the Naktong, North to the Yalu (June–November, 1950)* (Washington, D.C.: Office of the Chief of Military History, Department of the Army, 1961); Carl Berger, *The Korea Knot: A Military-Political History* (Philadelphia: University of Pennsylvania Press, 1957); Cumings, *The Origins of the Korean War*; Bruce Cumings, ed., *Child of Conflict: The Korean-American Relationship, 1943–1953* (Seattle: University of Washington Press, 1983); Harold Joyce Noble, *Embassy at War* (Seattle: University of Washington Press, 1975); David Rees, *Korea: The Limited War* (New York: St. Martin's Press, 1964); John W. Riley and Wilbur Schramm, *The Reds Take a City: The Communist Occupation of Seoul, with Eyewitness Accounts* (New Brunswick, N.J.: Rutgers University Press, 1951); Michael C. Sandusky, *America's Parallel* (Alexandria: Old Dominion Press, 1983); and I. F. Stone, *The Hidden History of the Korean War* (New York: Monthly Review Press, 1952).

59. According to available accounts, the initial decision to draw a line at the thirty-eighth parallel was made on August 10–11, 1945, by the United States in an all-night session of the State-War-Navy Coordinating Committee (SWNCC) four days prior to the end of World War II. According to Bruce Cumings, by a general order, Col. Charles H. Bonesteel and Maj. Dean Rusk were asked to come up with a plan to define the zones to be occupied in Korea by American and Russian forces. They were allowed only thirty minutes to come up with the plan to be presented to the SWNCC. Without time for careful thought and deliberation, they hastily drew a line following the thirty-eighth parallel, which allowed an almost even division of the Korean peninsula. Seoul, the largest city in Korea and also its capital from during the Yi dynasty through the period of Japanese colonial rule, was included in the southern part which put it under the control of the United States. See Cumings, *The Origins of the Korean War*, 120. See also John Gunther, *The Riddle of MacArthur* (New York: Harper and Brothers, 1950), 178; and Sandusky, *America's Parallel*, 226–227.

60. The contents of the accounts of Tomoo Morita, a Japanese foreign office staffer, were quoted from Republic of Korea National Red Cross, *The Dispersed Families*, 49.

61. Ibid., 55–56.

62. Ibid., 58.

63. A full text of the agreement on the north-south mail exchange is in ibid., 54–55.

64. Ibid., 55.

65. Ibid., 61.

66. *Chosun Ilbo*, July 22, 1947.

67. According to the posthumously published memoirs of Yun-yŏng Lee, who was minister of health and welfare at the time of the war and later elevated to the position of deputy prime minister in the Rhee administration, President Rhee's optimism was misguided by his defense minister, Sŏng-mo Shin. See *Shin Dong-A*, 297 (June 1984): 198–224.

68. "The Soviet representative on the Security Council, having avoided the meetings which denounced the aggression in Korea, attempted to label the Security Council resolution illegal because of his absence. However, since the Security Council had determined that mere absence did not constitute a veto, the North Korean regime and its communist accomplices stood accused before the bar of world opinion as aggressors" (U.S. Department of the Army, *Korea—1950* [Washington, D.C.: U.S. Government Printing Office, 1952], 11).

69. Ibid.

70. Republic of Korea National Red Cross, *The Dispersed Families*, 74–75.

71. Ibid., 76.

72. Allen S. Whiting, *China Crosses the Yalu: The Decision to Enter the Korean War* (Stanford: Stanford University Press, 1960), 118.

73. John Miller, Jr., Owen J. Carroll, and Margaret E. Tackley, *Korea, 1951–1953* (Washington, D.C.: U.S. Government Printing Office, 1956), 4.

74. Republic of Korea National Red Cross, *The Dispersed Families*, 79–80.

75. Ibid., 81.

76. Ibid.
77. Ibid., 80.
78. Ibid., 81–82.
79. Ibid., 83.
80. Ibid., 84.
81. For further details on General MacArthur's release, see Trumbull Higgins, *Korea and the Fall of MacArthur: A Precis in Limited War* (New York: Oxford University Press, 1960); and Gunther, *The Riddle of MacArthur.*
82. This was after the United States had halted two large communist attacks, and the ground war was in a lull. On May 30 Gen. Matthew Ridgway reported to Washington that the enemy had suffered heavy casualties. Ridgway believed the military situation in Korea would offer optimum advantages in support of diplomatic negotiation. See Barton J. Bernstein, "The Struggle over the Korean Armistice: Prisoners of Repatriation?" in *Child of Conflict: The Korean-American Relationship, 1943–1953,* edited by Bruce Cumings (Seattle: University of Washington Press, 1983), 262–263.

Chapter 3. Korean Family and Kinship

1. Hesung Chun Koh has provided a comprehensive bibliographic guide on Korean kinship and family, with a special section on women. See Hesung Chun Koh, *Korean Family and Kinship Studies Guide* (New Haven: Human Relations Area Files, 1980).
2. Francis L. K. Hsu, "Kinship is the Key," *Center Magazine,* 6 (1973): 4–14.
3. In the distinctly hierarchical social system in Korea since the Yi dynasty, *yangban* refers to nobles. See Vincent S. R. Brandt, *A Korean Village: Between Farm and Sea* (Cambridge: Harvard University Press, 1971), 11–12; Takashi Hatada, *A History of Korea,* edited and translated by Warren W. Smith, Jr., and Benjamin H. Hazard (Santa Barbara, Calif.: American Bibliographical Center, 1969), 103; and Cornelius Osgood, *The Koreans and Their Culture* (New York: Ronald Press, 1951), 44.
4. Choong Soon Kim, "The Yon'jul-hon or Chain-string Form of Marriage Arrangement in Korea," *Journal of Marriage and the Family,* 36 (1974): 579.
5. See *Hankook Ilbo,* February 29, 1984.
6. Chu-su Kim, *Ch'injok sangsokbŏp* (Kinship and inheritance laws) (Seoul: Pŏbmun-sa, 1983), 111–112.
7. Kwang-kyu Lee, *Han'guk kajok ŭi kujo punsŏk* (A structural analysis of the Korean family) (Seoul: Ilchi-sa, 1982), 117.
8. Roger L. Janelli and Dawnhee Yim Janelli, *Ancestor Worship and Korean Society* (Stanford: Stanford University Press, 1982), 40.
9. Francis L. K. Hsu, *Americans and Chinese: Purpose and Fulfillment in Great Civilizations* (Garden City: Natural History Press, 1970), 78.
10. William E. Henthorn, *A History of Korea* (New York: Free Press, 1971), 66–67.

11. In-hak Choi, *A Type Index of Korean Folktales* (Seoul: Myong Ji University Press, 1979), 163–176.

12. Janelli and Janelli, *Ancestor Worship*, 50.

13. Ibid., 51.

14. Ibid., 36.

15. Youngsook Kim Harvey, *Six Korean Women: The Socialization of Shamans* (St. Paul: West Publishing Co., 1979), 63, 260–269.

16. Janelli and Janelli, *Ancestor Worship*, 13. See also Kwang-kyu Lee, "Tongjok chiptan kwa chosang sungbae (Descent group and ancestor worship)," *Han'guk munhwa illyuhak* (Korean cultural anthropology), 9 (1977): 13; and Martina Deuchler, "The Tradition: Women during the Yi Dynasty," in *Virtues in Conflict: Tradition and the Korean Woman Today*, edited by Sandra Mattielli (Seoul: Royal Asiatic Society, Korean Branch, 1977), 29.

17. Clark W. Sorensen, "Women, Men; Inside, Outside: The Division of Labor in Rural Central Korea," in *Korean Women: View from the Inner Room*, edited by Laurel Kendall and Mark Peterson (New Haven: East Rock Press, 1983), 64.

18. A comprehensive body of administrative and criminal law of the Ming dynasty of China, which was published in 1397.

19. See Kwang-kyu Lee, *Han'guk kajok ŭi sajŏk yŏngu* (A historical study of the Korean family) (Seoul: Ilchi-sa, 1983), 250–251; and Yung-chung Kim, ed. and trans., *Women of Korea: A History from Ancient Times to 1945* (Seoul: Ewha Womans University Press, 1979), 100.

20. See Chu-su Kim, *Ch'injok sangsokbŏp*, 163–168.

21. See T'ae-yŏng Lee, *Han'guk ihon chaedo yŏngu* (A study of divorce in Korea) (Seoul: Yŏsŏng Munjae Yŏnguwŏn, 1957).

22. Jai-seuk Choi, *Han'guk kajok yŏngu* (A study of the Korean family) (Seoul: Minjung-sŏgwan, 1966), 405–407.

23. Janelli and Janelli, *Ancestor Worship*, 10. See also Osgood, *The Koreans*, 242.

24. Sang-bok Han, "Han'guk ingugwajŏngae kwanhan illyuhakjŏk yŏngu (An anthropological study of Korean population processes)," *Han'guk munhwa illyuhak* (Korean cultural anthropology), 9 (1977): 167–174.

25. In earlier times Korean adoption was not so rigidly agnatic. Sisters' sons, daughters' sons, wives' natal kin, and even nonkin were appointed heirs. But this changed to a strict agnatic rule over the last few hundred years. See Mark Peterson, "Some Korean Attitudes Toward Adoption," *Korea Journal*, 17 (1977): 28–31; and Lee, *Han'guk kajok ŭi sajŏk yŏngu*, 328.

26. In Japan, for instance, if there was no son, a son-in-law could be technically adopted into the family at the time of his marriage. "If a family had a daughter but no sons, the man (probably a younger son) who married the daughter ordinarily would take over the family name and continue the *ie* [household]" (Ezra F. Vogel, "The Japanese Family," in *Comparative Family Systems*, edited by M. F. Nimkoff [Boston: Houghton Mifflin Co., 1965], 288). This Japanese practice is rare in Korea and is not considered ideal: "It was not practiced before the Japanese period, and it has been practiced only rarely since; those who have practiced it in recent years seem to be ashamed of it" (Hesung Chun Koh, "Korean Women, Conflict, and

Change: An Approach to Development Planning," in *Korean Women: View from the Inner Room*, edited by Laurel Kendall and Mark Peterson [New Haven: East Rock Press, 1983], 165). See also Arthur P. Wolf and Chieh-shan Haung, *Marriage and Adoption in China, 1845–1945* (Stanford: Stanford University Press, 1980).

27.   A clan is a kin group whose members believe themselves to be descended from common ancestors. It refers to a kind of compromise kin group based on a rule of residence and a rule of descent following the line of George P. Murdock and John Gillin. As Murdock admitted, there are difficulties involved in a definition of clan. Raymond Firth defines clan as a grouping composed of a number of lineages. If we follow the definition of Firth, the *munjung* is closer to lineage than clan. In this way, a *ssijok* or *ch'injok* is composed of many *munjungs,* or lineages. See Raymond Firth, *We, the Tikopia* (London: George Allen and Unwin, 1936), 53; John Gillin, *The Ways of Men* (New York: Appleton-Century-Crofts, 1948), 439; Choong Soon Kim, "The Yon'jul-hon," 575–579; George P. Murdock, *Social Structure* (New York: Macmillan Co., 1949), 66–67; and A. R. Radcliffe-Brown and D. Forde, eds., *African Systems of Kinship and Marriage* (New York: Oxford University Press, 1950), 39–40.

28.   Choong Soon Kim, "The Yon'jul-hon," 576–577.

29.   An individual having the same surname is not necessarily a member of the same patrilineal clan. Korean name groups are divided into scores of clans, each distinguished by a prefatory name, for example, Andong Kim, Kyŏngju Kim, and so on. Andong and Kyŏngju indicate traditional places of origin.

30.   Edward W. Wagner has studied Korean genealogy. See Edward W. Wagner, "The Korean Chokpo as a Historical Source," in *Studies on Asian Genealogy*, edited by S. J. Palmer (Provo, Utah: Brigham Young University Press, 1971), 141–252; idem, "Two Early Genealogies and Women's Status in Early Yi Dynasty Korea," in *Korean Women: View from the Inner Room*, edited by Laurel Kendall and Mark Peterson (New Haven: East Rock Press, 1983), 23–32.

31.   See Choong Soon Kim, "Functional Analysis of Korean Kinship System" (Master's thesis, Emory University, 1968), 73–78.

32.   Ki-baik Lee, *A New History of Korea,* translated by Edward W. Wagner and Edward J. Shultz (Seoul: Ilchokak, 1984), 217–218.

33.   Choong Soon Kim, "Adaptive Mode of Korean Immigrants in a Southern City," in *Urban Anthropology in Tennessee*, edited by Billye S. Fogleman (Tennessee Anthropological Association, Miscellaneous Paper, no. 4, 1980), 6. See Ilsoo Kim, *New Urban Immigrants: The Korean Community in New York* (Princeton: Princeton University Press, 1981), 199–201; Won Moo Hurh and Kwang Chung Kim, *Korean Immigrants in America: A Structural Analysis of Ethnic Confinement and Adhesive Adaptation* (Rutherford, N.J.: Fairleigh Dickinson University Press, 1984), 88.

34.   See Sang-bok Han, *Korean Fisherman: Ecological Adaptation in Three Communities* (Seoul: Seoul National University Press, 1977), 55.

35.   Chu-su Kim, *Ch'injok sangsokbŏp*, 41–42.

36.   Ibid., 410–414.

37.   Francis L. K. Hsu includes these characteristics in his "father-son" dominant dyad. See Hsu, "The Effect of Dominant Kinship Relationships; *Current*

Anthropology, 8 (1967): 512–517; Hsu, *Kinship and Culture*; and Hsu, *Rugged Individualism,* 217–247.

38. Hsu, *Kinship and Culture,* 11.

39. See the full list of morphological characteristics of a fertile woman and a barren woman in Kyu-t'ae Lee, *Han'guk-in ŭi ŭishik kujo* (Structure of Korean thought patterns), 2 vols. (Seoul: Munri-sa, 1981), 2: 370–371.

40. A full text of the interview with Su-kwan Sim by Sŏng-han Kim is in *Shin Dong-A,* 228 (July 1984): 438–450.

41. W. J. Cash, *The Mind of the South* (New York: Alfred A. Knopf, 1941), x.

Chapter 4. An Elderly Mother Longs for Her Son

1. The *sangmin* (also known as *yangmin* or *sangnom*) was a distinct social class during the Yi dynasty; farmers, merchants, and artisans were considered commoners. See Henderson, *Korea,* 50–55.

2. See Choong Soon Kim, "Changing Patterns of Korean Names and Acculturation," *Working Papers in Sociology and Anthropology,* 3 (1969): 24–25.

3. See Osgood, *The Koreans,* 50.

4. See D. L. Guemple, "Saunik: Name Sharing as a Factor Governing Eskimo Kinship Terms," *Ethnology,* 4 (1965): 325. Another interesting study on Korean naming patterns is Kyu-hyŏn Lee, *Irŭm* (Name) (Seoul: Pŏmhan Ch'ulp'an-sa, 1967).

5. Yung-chung Kim, *Women of Korea,* 52.

6. See Hsu, *Americans and Chinese,* 78; Janelli and Janelli, *Ancestor Worship,* 50–51; and In-hak Choi, *A Type Index of Korean Folktales,* 163–176.

7. Sorensen, "Patterns of Misinformation."

8. T'ae-gil Kim, *Sosŏl munhakae natanatanan han'guk-in ŭi kach'ikwan* (Korean values as reflected in the Korean novel) (Seoul: Ilchi-sa, 1980), 101–103.

Chapter 5. Dispersed Spouses

1. "In 1915 there were 56,253 elementary school boys and 5,976 elementary school girls. In secondary schools, one third of the whole student body were girls: 822 boys and 250 girls" (Yung-chung Kim, *Women of Korea,* 233).

2. See William J. Goode, *World Revolution and Family Patterns* (New York: Free Press, 1970), 28.

3. See Donald M. Seekins, "The Society and Its Environment," in *North Korea: A Country Study (Area Handbook Series),* edited by Frederica M. Bunge (Washington, D.C.: U.S. Government Printing Office, 1981), 76.

4. Ibid., 81.

5. Ibid., 79.

6. See Vogel, "The Japanese Family," 292–293.

7. This examination is similar to the *kwagŏ* of the Yi dynasty. The *kwagŏ* was

given to those who wanted to serve as civil servants in any branch of government; it asked questions on the Confucian classics. The *kodŭng kosi* or *kosi* had two exams, one for public administration and the other for the judiciary, which were concerned exclusively with specific knowledge of these fields.

8.   See Choong Soon Kim, "Functional Analysis," 37–44.

9.   See Peter Hyun, *Darkness at Dawn: A North Korean Diary* (Seoul: Hanjin Publishing Co., 1981), 10.

10.   See C. I. Eugene Kim and B. C. Koh, eds., *Journey to North Korea: Personal Perceptions*, Research Papers and Policy Studies, no. 8 (Berkeley: Institute of East Asian Studies, 1983); see also Andrew C. Nam, *North Korea: Her Past, Reality, and Impression* (Kalamazoo: Center for Korean Studies, Western Michigan University, 1978).

11.   See Hatada, *A History of Korea*, 125.

12.   Helen Rose Tieszen, a Methodist-Mennonite missionary and educator, has made an interesting study, collecting, analyzing, and translating 135 Korean proverbs that most succinctly express attitudes about Korean women; the terse statements express fixed beliefs of Koreans. See Helen Rose Tieszen, "Korean Proverbs about Women," in *Virtues in Conflict: Tradition and the Korean Woman Today*, edited by Sandra Mattielli (Seoul: Royal Asiatic Society, Korean Branch, 1977), 57.

13.   Tieszen reports a similar proverb: "The old man has three measures of lice; the widow has three measures of silver" (ibid., 63).

Chapter 6. A Man Longs for His Parents

1.   Tales of *myŏng-t'ae* are available in *Myŏngch'ŏn kunji* (History of Myŏngch'ŏn County) (Seoul: Myŏngch'ŏn County Historical Commission, 1981), 165–166.

2.   See Janelli and Janelli, *Ancestor Worship*, 94.

3.   Janelli and Janelli describe this tablet in detail, showing a photograph of the classic wooden tablet in their book (ibid., 94). See also Kwang-kyu Lee, "Tongjok chiptan kwa chosang sungbae," 10.

4.   Discrimination against former landlords is discussed in Seekins, "The Society," 76.

5.   John Merrill, "Internal Warfare in Korea, 1948–1950," in *Child of Conflict: The Korean-American Relationship, 1943–1953*, edited by Bruce Cumings (Seattle: University of Washington Press, 1983), 137.

6.   See Chong-sik Lee, *The Politics of Korean Nationalism* (Berkeley: University of California Press, 1965), ix; Dae-sook Suh, *The Korean Communist Movement, 1918–1948* (Princeton: Princeton University Press, 1967), 132; and Robert A. Scalapino and Chong-sik Lee, *Communism in Korea*, 2 pts. (Berkeley: University of California Press, 1972), pt. 1, chaps. 1–3.

7.   The logic and figures for calculating the distance from one kin to another in a given kin group are shown in Kwang-kyu Lee and Youngsook Kim Harvey, "Teknonymy and Geonomy in Korean Kinship Terminology," *Ethnology*, 12

(1973): 32–33. See also Janelli and Janelli, *Ancestor Worship*, 106–110; and Choong Soon Kim, "Functional Analysis," 23–24.

8.   Kwang-kyu Lee and Harvey, "Teknonymy and Geononymy," 41.

9.   See the contents of Korean genealogies in Wagner, "Two Early Genealogies," 23–32.

10.   "The name of a family" other than the surname is also used in Tikopia. See Raymond Firth, "Family in Tikopia," in *Comparative Family Systems*, edited by M. F. Nimkoff (Boston: Houghton Mifflin Co., 1965), 107.

11.   Choong Soon Kim, "Functional Analysis," 58–59.

12.   Kwang-kyu Lee and Harvey, "Teknonymy and Geononymy," 41.

13.   See an example of the functions of public property owned by a clan in Choong Soon Kim, "Functional Analysis," 73–78.

Chapter 7. The Reunion Movement
and the Reunion Telethon

1.   Detailed accounts of voluntary repatriation in the exchange of prisoners of war are in Bernstein, "The Struggle over the Korean Armistice," 261–307.

2.   In early 1952, before a careful screening could be done, the Far East command at P'anmunjŏm predicted that approximately 116,000 of 132,000 prisoners of war in United Nations custody and 18,000 of 38,000 civilian internees would desire repatriation to North Korea. But on April 19 the American delegation informed the communists that only 70,000 instead of 116,000 would be returned. The communists were embarrassed and so was the United Nations delegation. "Despite official American denials, some of Chiang's troops [Republic of China] were actually used as guards in the Chinese camps and they helped establish a reign of terror there. . . . When the Nationalist leaders in the prison compound asked who wished to return to the PRC, Joy recorded in his diary, 'those doing so were either beaten black and blue or killed.' . . . the majority of the POWs were too terrified to frankly express their choice" (Bernstein, "The Struggle over the Korean Armistice," 285).

3.   Republic of Korea National Red Cross, *The Dispersed Families*, 90.

4.   Korean contact with the ICRC has a rather long history, going back to the Yi dynasty. See Eun-bum Choe, *Chŏkshipja wa indobŏp* (The Red Cross and humanitarian law) (Seoul: Republic of Korea National Red Cross, 1983), 14–15.

5.   The limitation of the ICRC was also apparent in 1951 in an investigation of the use of germ warfare by North Korea. See David P. Forsythe, *Humanitarian Politics: The International Committee of the Red Cross* (Baltimore: Johns Hopkins University Press, 1977), 43.

6.   On August 16, 1966, adhering to the 1949 Geneva convention, the ICRC recognized the Republic of Korea National Red Cross (South Korean Red Cross). Ibid, 13.

7.   Republic of Korea National Red Cross, *The Dispersed Families*, 91.

8.   The resolution on dispersed families adopted by the eighteenth international conference was reaffirmed again at the nineteenth conference in New Delhi

in 1957, at the twentieth conference in Vienna in 1965, and at other international meetings, such as the league's board of governors' in Mexico City in 1971. In addition, in 1974 a conference on reuniting dispersed families was held in Florence, and the topic was raised at the conference on security and cooperation in Helsinki in 1975.

9. Regarding the number of registrants, different sources have slightly different figures. See *Dong-A Ilbo, Ah! Sara issŏttguna* (Oh! You were alive after all) (Seoul: Dong-A Ilbo, 1983), 284.

10. Republic of Korea National Red Cross, *The Dispersed Families*, 92.

11. *Dong-A Ilbo*, February 2, 1971.

12. Republic of Korea National Red Cross, *The Dispersed Families*, 187. Regarding these prerequisites: "Park's 'U.N. effort' clause was, however, abandoned for all practical purposes when the much celebrated North-South Joint Communiqué of July 1972 was announced" (Yang, *Korea and Two Regimes*, 319).

13. Republic of Korea National Red Cross, *The Dispersed Families*, 225.

14. See Sang-wu Lee, "Nambuk chojŏl hoedam (South-North Coordinating Committee)," *Shin Dong-A*, 228 (August 1983): 202–229.

15. The text of the communiqué is in Se-jin Kim, ed., *Korean Unification: Source Materials with an Introduction* (Seoul: Research Center for Peace and Unification, 1976), 319.

16. Republic of Korea National Red Cross, *The Dispersed Families*, 249.

17. "At lunar New Year and the Harvest Moon Festival (*ch'usŏk*), the major holidays of the year, many emigrant kinsmen and their families would return to the village for the festivities and ancestor rituals" (Janelli and Janelli, *Ancestor Worship*, 26).

18. Byung Chul Koh, *The Foreign Policy of North Korea* (New York: Frederick A. Praeger, 1969), 112–157. Also referred to as the peaceful unification policy; see Soon Sung Cho, "The Politics of North Korea's Unification Policies, 1950–1965," *World Politics*, 19 (1967): 218–241.

19. Two additional tunnels were found in March 1975 and October 1978.

20. See a comparison of the original proposals by Seoul and P'yŏngyang in *Korea Newsreview*, July 20, 1985, p. 4.

21. See ibid., August 31, 1985, p. 7.

22. See the editorial in *Hankook Ilbo*, September 23, 1985.

23. *The Korea Times English Section*, September 23, 1985.

24. See Republic of Korea National Red Cross, *The Dispersed Families*, 209–210. Of the 135 reunited families 5 were not identified.

25. Ibid., 210.

26. For further details, see Korean Broadcasting System, *Isan kajok ŭl ch'at'ssŭp nida* (The search for dispersed families) (Seoul: KBS, 1984).

27. Criticism and suggestions by citizens of South Korea are in the *Dong-A Ilbo*, July 5, 1983, including its editorial of July 5, 1983; see also *Dong-A Ilbo, Ah! Sara issŏttguna*, 264–266.

28. *Dong-A Ilbo, Ah! Sara issŏttguna*, 158.

29. See *Hankook Ilbo*, June 13, 25; July 2, 9, 16, 23, 1984.

30. See *Hankook Ilbo*, July 4, 1983.

31. *Dong-A Ilbo, Ah! Sara issŏttguna*, 268–270.

32. Over the same period Burma's average annual growth was 1.0 percent, India's 1.4 percent, Pakistan's 2.8 percent, Indonesia's 4.1 percent, and the Philippines' 2.6 percent. See David I. Steinberg, "Development Lessons from the Korean Experience—A Review Article," *Journal of Asian Studies*, 42 (1982): 91.

33. Ibid.; see also Karl Moskowitz, "Korean Development and Korean Studies —A Review Article," *Journal of Asian Studies*, 42 (1982): 63–90.

34. See Robert H. Lauer, *Perspectives on Social Change* (Boston: Allyn and Bacon, 1982), 156–180.

35. *Hankook Ilbo*, June 5, 1983.

36. *Dong-A Ilbo, Ah! Sara issŏttguna*, 279.

37. Sung Chul Yang, "Socialist Education in North Korea," in *Journey to North Korea: Personal Perceptions*, edited by C. I. Eugene Kim and B. C. Koh, Research Papers and Policy Studies, no. 8 (Berkeley: Institute of East Asian Studies, 1983), 69.

Chapter 8. Reunited Families

1. *Dong-A Ilbo, Ah! Sara issŏttguna*, 290.

2. Eugene Irving Knez, "Sam Jong Dong: A South Korean Village" (Ph.D. dissertation, Syracuse University, 1959), 70.

3. John F. Embree, *Suye Mura: A Japanese Village* (Chicago: University of Chicago Press, 1939), 213–214.

4. Janelli and Janelli, *Ancestor Worship*, 44. See also Dawnhee Yim Janelli, "Logical Contradictions in Korean Learned Fortunetelling" (Ph.D. dissertation, University of Pennsylvania, 1977).

Chapter 9. Faithful Endurance

1. *The Fulton Daily Leader*, September 7, 1983.

2. Young Whan Kihl, "The Issue of Korean Unification," in *Journey to North Korea: Personal Perceptions*, edited by C. I. Eugene Kim and B. C. Koh, Research Papers and Policy Studies, no. 8 (Berkeley: Institute of East Asian Studies, 1983), III.

3. Manwoo Lee, "How North Korea Sees Itself," in *Journey to North Korea: Personal Perceptions*, edited by C. I. Eugene Kim and B. C. Koh, Research Papers and Policy Studies, no. 8 (Berkeley: Institute of East Asian Studies, 1983), 138.

4. Henderson, *Korea*, 13.

5. See Yun-sik Kim, ed., *Isan, pundanmunhak taep'yo sosŏl chip* (Selected novels on family separation and literature on partition) (Seoul: Dong-A Ilbo, 1983).

6. *Dong-A Ilbo*, July 6, 1983.

7. Choong Soon Kim, "The Korean Value System Reflected in a Fortune-

telling Book" (Paper presented at the eighty-second annual meeting of the American Anthropological Association, Chicago, November 16–20, 1983).

8.   Laurel Kendall, *Shamans, Housewives, and Other Restless Spirits: Women in Korean Ritual Life* (Honolulu: University of Hawaii Press, 1985), 202.

9.   *Dong-A Ilbo*, July 6, 1983; *Hankook Ilbo*, July 9, 1983; *Hankook Ilbo*, March 27, 1984.

10.   Choong Soon Kim, "Can an Anthropologist Go Home Again?" *American Anthropologist*, 89 (1987): 943–945.

11.   Richardson, "Anthropologist—The Myth Teller," 530.

Selected Bibliography

Aceves, Joseph. *Social Change in a Spanish Village*. Cambridge, Mass.: Schenkman Publishing Co., 1971.

————."Competence by Blood: Ethnological Fieldwork in the Ancestral Village." Paper presented at the seventy-seventh annual meeting of the American Anthropological Association, Los Angeles, November 14–18, 1978.

Aguilar, John L. "Inside Research: An Ethnography of a Debate." In *Anthropologists at Home in North America: Methods and Issues in the Study of One's Own Society*, edited by Donald A. Messerschmidt, 15–26. New York: Cambridge University Press, 1981.

Appleman, Roy E. *United States Army in the Korean War: South to the Naktong, North to the Yalu (June–November, 1950)*. Washington, D.C.: Office of the Chief of Military History, Department of the Army, 1961.

Befu, Harumi. *Japan: An Anthropological Introduction*. New York: Thomas Y. Crowell, 1971.

Berger, Carl. *The Korea Knot: A Military-Political History*. Philadelphia: University of Pennsylvania Press, 1957.

Bernstein, Barton J. "The Struggle over the Korean Armistice: Prisoners of Repatriation?" In *Child of Conflict: The Korean-American Relationship, 1943–1953*, edited by Bruce Cumings, 261–307. Seattle: University of Washington Press, 1983.

Berry, Mary Elizabeth. *Hideyoshi*. Cambridge: Harvard University Press, 1982.

Brandt, Vincent S. R. *A Korean Village: Between Farm and Sea*. Cambridge: Harvard University Press, 1971.

Cash, W. J. *The Mind of the South*. New York: Alfred A. Knopf, 1941.

Cassell, Joan, and Murray L. Wax, eds. "Ethical Problems of Fieldwork." *Social Problems*, 27 (1980): 259–378.

Chilungu, Simeon W. "Issues in the Ethics of Research Method: An Interpretation of the Anglo-American Perspective." *Current Anthropology*, 17 (1976): 457–481.

Cho, Soon Sung. "The Politics of North Korea's Unification Policies, 1950–1965." *World Politics*, 19 (1967): 218–241.

Choe, Eun-bum. *Chŏkshipja wa indobŏp* (The Red Cross and humanitarian law). Seoul: Republic of Korea National Red Cross, 1983.

Choi, In-hak. *A Type Index of Korean Folktales*. Seoul: Myong Ji University Press, 1979.

Choi, Jai-seuk. *Han'guk kajok yŏngu* (A study of the Korean family). Seoul: Minjung-sŏgwan, 1966.

Cumings, Bruce. *The Origins of the Korean War: Liberation and the Emergence of Separate Regimes 1945–1947*. Princeton: Princeton University Press, 1981.

———, ed. *Child of Conflict: The Korean-American Relationship, 1943–1953*. Seattle: University of Washington Press, 1983.

Current Anthropology, 8 (1967): 512–517.

Dalton, M. *Men Who Manage*. New York: Wiley, 1959.

Deuchler, Martina. "The Tradition: Women during the Yi Dynasty." In *Virtues in Conflict: Tradition and the Korean Woman Today*, edited by Sandra Mattielli, 1–47. Seoul: Royal Asiatic Society, Korean Branch, 1977.

Dong-A Ilbo. Ah! Sara issŏttguna: Isan kajok ŭi pigŭk kwa chaehoe ŭi aechŏlhan sayŏn dŭl (Oh! You were alive after all: The sad stories of family dispersal and the vivid accounts of the family reunions). Seoul: Dong-A Ilbo, 1983.

Embree, John F. *Suye Mura: A Japanese Village*. Chicago: University of Chicago Press, 1939.

Fei, Xiatong. "Toward a People's Anthropology." *Human Organization*, 39 (1980): 115–120.

Fernandez, James W. "Reflections on Looking into Mirrors." *Semiotica*, 30 (1980): 27–39.

———. *Bwiti: An Ethnography of the Religious Imagination in Africa*. Princeton: Princeton University Press, 1982.

Firth, Raymond. *We, the Tikopia*. London: George Allen and Unwin, 1936.

———. "Family in Tikopia." In *Comparative Family Systems*, edited by M. F. Nimkoff, 105–120. Boston: Houghton Mifflin Co., 1965.

Forsythe, David P. *Humanitarian Politics: The International Committee of the Red Cross*. Baltimore: Johns Hopkins University Press, 1977.

Gane, William J. *Repatriation: From 25 September 1945 to 31 December 1945*. Seoul: U.S. Military Government in Korea, 1947.

Gillin, John. *The Ways of Men*. New York: Appleton-Century-Crofts, 1948.

Goode, William J. *World Revolution and Family Patterns*. New York: Free Press, 1970.

Goodenough, Ward. "Componential Analysis and The Study of Meaning." *Language*, 32 (1956): 195–216.

Grajdanzev, Andrew J. *Modern Korea*. New York: Octagon Books, 1978.

Guemple, D. L. "Saunik: Name Sharing as a Factor Governing Eskimo Kinship Terms." *Ethnology*, 4 (1965): 323–335.

Gunther, John. *The Riddle of MacArthur*. New York: Harper and Brothers, 1950.

Gwaltney, John L. "Common Sense and Science: Urban Core Black Observations." In *Anthropologists at Home in North America: Methods and Issues in the Study of One's Own Society*, edited by Donald A. Messerschmidt, 46–61. New York: Cambridge University Press, 1981.

Han, Sang-bok. *Korean Fisherman: Ecological Adaptation in Three Communities*. Seoul: Seoul National University Press, 1977.

————. "Han'guk ingugwajŏngae kwanhan illyuhakjŏk yŏngu (An anthropological study of Korean population processes)." *Han'guk munhwa illyuhak* (Korean cultural anthropology), 9 (1977): 167–174.

Han, Woo-keun. *The History of Korea*. Seoul: Eul-yoo Publishing Co., 1981.

Harvey, Youngsook Kim. *Six Korean Women: The Socialization of Shamans*. St. Paul: West Publishing Co., 1979.

Hatada, Takashi. *A History of Korea*. Edited and translated by Warren W. Smith, Jr., and Benjamin H. Hazard. Santa Barbara, Calif.: American Bibliographical Center, 1969.

Henderson, Gregory. *Korea: The Politics of the Vortex*. Cambridge: Harvard University Press, 1968.

Hennigh, Lawrence. "The Anthropologist as Key Informant: Inside a Rural Oregon Town." In *Anthropologists at Home in North America: Methods and Issues in the Study of One's Own Society*, edited by Donald A. Messerschmidt, 121–132. New York: Cambridge University Press, 1981.

Henthorn, William E. *A History of Korea*. New York: Free Press, 1971.

Hicks, George L. "Informant Anonymity and Scientific Accuracy: The Problem of Pseudonyms." *Human Organization*, 36 (1977): 214–220.

Higgins, Trumbull. *Korea and the Fall of MacArthur: A Précis in Limited War*. New York: Oxford University Press, 1960.

Hsu, Francis L. K. "The Effect of Dominant Kinship Relationships on Kin and Non-Kin Behavior: A Hypothesis." *American Anthropologist*, 67 (1965): 638–661.

————. *Americans and Chinese: Purpose and Fulfillment in Great Civilizations*. Garden City, N.Y.: Natural History Press, 1970.

————. "Kinship is the Key." *Center Magazine*, 6 (1973): 4–14.

————. *Rugged Individualism Reconsidered: Essays in Psychological Anthropology*. Knoxville: University of Tennessee Press, 1983.

————, ed. *Kinship and Culture*. Chicago: Aldine Publishing Co., 1971.

Hurh, Won Moo, and Kwang Chung Kim. *Korean Immigrants in America: A Structural Analysis of Ethnic Confinement and Adhesive Adaptation*. Rutherford, N.J.: Fairleigh Dickinson University Press, 1984.

Hyun, Kyoo-whan. *Han'guk iyumin-sa* (A history of Korean wanderers and emigrants). 2 vols. Seoul: Ŏmunkak, 1967.

Hyun, Peter. *Darkness at Dawn: A North Korean Diary*. Seoul: Hanjin Publishing Co., 1981.

Hyun, Ung [Peter] and Pong-hak Hyun. *Chung-gong ŭi han'in tŭl* (Koreans in the People's Republic of China). Seoul: Pŏmyang-sa, 1984.

James, Edwin. *The Thirty Years of Indian Captivity of John Tanner.* Minneapolis: Ross and Haines, 1956.

Janelli, Dawnhee Yim. "Logical Contradictions in Korean Learned Fortunetelling." Ph.D. dissertation, University of Pennsylvania, 1977.

Janelli, Roger L., and Dawnhee Yim Janelli. *Ancestor Worship and Korean Society.* Stanford: Stanford University Press, 1982.

Kendall, Laurel. *Shamans, Housewives, and Other Restless Spirits: Women in Korean Ritual Life.* Honolulu: University of Hawaii Press, 1985.

Kidder, Edward. *Prehistoric Japanese Arts: Jomon Pottery.* Palo Alto: Kodansha International, 1968.

Kihl, Young Whan. "The Issue of Korean Unification." In *Journey to North Korea: Personal Perceptions,* edited by C. I. Eugene Kim and B. C. Koh. Research Papers and Policy Studies, no. 8, 99–117. Berkeley: Institute of East Asian Studies, 1983.

Kim, C. I. Eugene, and B. C. Koh, eds. *Journey to North Korea: Personal Perceptions.* Research Papers and Policy Studies, no. 8. Berkeley: Institute of East Asian Studies, 1983.

Kim, Choong Soon. "Functional Analysis of Korean Kinship System." Master's thesis, Emory University, Atlanta, 1968.

———. "Changing Patterns of Korean Names and Acculturation." *Working Papers in Sociology and Anthropology,* 3 (1969): 24–31.

———. "The Yon'jul-hon or Chain-string Form of Marriage Arrangement in Korea." *Journal of Marriage and the Family,* 36 (1974): 575–579.

———. *An Asian Anthropologist in the South: Field Experiences with Blacks, Indians, and Whites.* Knoxville: University of Tennessee Press, 1977.

———. "Adaptive Mode of Korean Immigrants in a Southern City." In *Urban Anthropology in Tennessee,* edited by Billye S. Fogleman. Miscellaneous Paper, no. 4, 1–11. Tennessee Anthropological Association, 1980.

———. "The Korean Value System Reflected in a Fortune-telling Book." Paper presented at the eighty-second annual meeting of the American Anthropological Association, Chicago, November 16–20, 1983.

———. "Can an Anthropologist Go Home Again?" *American Anthropologist,* 89 (1987): 943–945.

Kim, Chu-su. *Ch'injok sangsokbŏp* (Kinship and inheritance laws). Seoul: Pŏbmun-sa, 1983.

Kim, Ilsoo. *New Urban Immigrants: The Korean Community in New York.* Princeton: Princeton University Press, 1981.

Kim, Se-jin., ed. *Korean Unification: Source Materials with an Introduction.* Seoul: Research Center for Peace and Unification, 1976.

Kim, T'ae-gil. *Sosŏl munhakae natanatanan han'guk-in ŭi kach'ikwan* (Korean values as reflected in the Korean novel). Seoul: Ilchi-sa, 1980.

Kim, Yun-sik., ed. *Isan, pundanmunhak taep'yo sosŏl chip* (Selected novels on family separation and literature on partition). Seoul: Dong-A Ilbo, 1983.

Kim, Yung-chung., ed. and trans. *Women of Korea: A History from Ancient Times to 1945*. Seoul: Ewha Womans University Press, 1979.

Kluckhohn, Clyde. *Mirror for Man: The Relation of Anthropology to Modern Life*. New York: McGraw-Hill, 1949.

Knez, Eugene Irving. "Sam Jong Dong: A South Korean Village." Ph.D. dissertation, Syracuse University, 1959.

Koh, Byung Chul. *The Foreign Policy of North Korea*. New York: Frederick A. Praeger, 1969.

Koh, Hesung Chun. *Korean Family and Kinship Studies Guide*. New Haven: Human Relations Area Files, 1980.

———. "Korean Women, Conflict, and Change: An Approach to Development Planning." In *Korean Women: View from the Inner Room*, edited by Laurel Kendall and Mark Peterson, 159–174. New Haven: East Rock Press, 1983.

Korean Broadcasting System. *Isan kajok ŭl ch'at'ssŭp nida: T.V. t'ŭkbyŏl sangbangsong 138-il ŭi kirok* (The search for dispersed families: Records of 138 days of a special live telecast). Seoul: KBS, 1984.

———. *Matta, maja, kŭrigo t'ong'gok haetta* (Correct, right, and wailed). Seoul: KBS, 1984.

Kuhn, Thomas S. *The Structure of Scientific Revolutions*. Chicago: University of Chicago Press, 1962.

Kuno, Yoshi S. *Japanese Expression on the Asiatic Continent*. 2 vols. Berkeley: University of California Press, 1937.

Langness, L. L. *The Life History in Anthropological Science*. New York: Holt, Rinehart and Winston, 1965.

Lauer, Robert H. *Perspectives on Social Change*. Boston: Allyn and Bacon, 1982.

Ledyard, Gari. "Galloping along with the Horseriders: Looking for the Founders of Japan." *Journal of Japanese Studies*, 2 (1976): 217–254.

Lee, Chae-Jin. *China's Korean Minority: The Politics of Ethnic Education*. Boulder: Westview Press, 1986.

Lee, Changsoo, and George DeVos. *Koreans in Japan: Ethnic Conflict and Accommodation*. Berkeley: University of California Press, 1981.

Lee, Chong-sik. *The Politics of Korean Nationalism*. Berkeley: University of California Press, 1965.

Lee, Ki-baik. *A New History of Korea*. Translated by Edward W. Wagner and Edward J. Shultz. Seoul: Ilchokak, 1984.

Lee, Kwang-kyu. "Tongjok chiptan kwa chosang sungbae (Descent group and ancestor worship)." *Han'guk munhwa illyuhak* (Korean cultural anthropology), 9 (1977): 1–24.

———. *Han'guk kajok ŭi kujo punsŏk* (A structural analysis of the Korean family). Seoul: Ilchi-sa, 1982.

———. *Han'guk kajok ŭi sajŏk yŏngu* (A historical study of the Korean family). Seoul: Ilchi-sa, 1983.

Lee, Kwang-kyu, and Youngsook Kim Harvey. "Teknonymy and Geononymy in Korean Kinship Terminology." *Ethnology*, 12 (1973): 31–46.

Lee, Kyu-hyŏn. *Irŭm* (Name). Seoul: Pŏmhan Ch'ulp'an-sa, 1967.

Lee, Kyu-t'ae. *Han'guk-in ŭi ŭishik kujo* (Structure of Korean thought patterns). 2 vols. Seoul: Munri-sa, 1981.

Lee, Manwoo. "How North Korea Sees Itself." In *Journey to North Korea: Personal Perceptions*, edited by C. I. Eugene Kim and B. C. Koh. Research Papers and Policy Studies, no. 8, 118–141. Berkeley: Institute of East Asian Studies, 1983.

Lee, Mun Woong. *Rural North Korea Under Communism: A Study of Socioeconomic Change*. Houston: Rice University Press, 1976.

————. "Kongsan ch'aejae ha'ae sŏŭi ch'injok chojik: Ibuk ŭi kyŏngu (Kinship organization under communism: A North Korean case study)." *Han'guk munhwa illyuhak* (Korean cultural anthropology), 9 (1977): 127–129.

Lee, T'ae-yŏng. *Han'guk ihon chaedo yŏngu* (A study of divorce in Korea). Seoul: Yŏsŏng Munjae Yŏnguwŏn, 1957.

McCune, Shannon. *Korea: The Land of Broken Calm*. New York: D. Van Nostrand, 1966.

Merrill, John. "Internal Warfare in Korea, 1948–1950." In *Child of Conflict: The Korean-American Relationship, 1943–1953*, edited by Bruce Cumings, 133–162. Seattle: University of Washington Press, 1983.

Messerschmidt, Donald A. "On Anthropology at Home." In *Anthropologists at Home in North America: Methods and Issues in the Study of One's Own Society*, edited by Donald A. Messerschmidt, 3–14. New York: Cambridge University Press, 1981.

————, ed. *Anthropologists at Home in North America: Methods and Issues in the Study of One's Own Society*. New York: Cambridge University Press, 1981.

Middleton, Harry J. *The Compact History of the Korean War*. New York: Hawthorn Books, 1965.

Miller, John, Jr., Owen J. Carroll, and Margaret E. Tackley. *Korea, 1951–1953*. Washington, D.C.: U.S. Government Printing Office, 1956.

Mitchell, Richard H. *The Korean Minority in Japan*. Berkeley: University of California Press, 1967.

Moskowitz, Karl. "Korean Development and Korean Studies—A Review Article." *Journal of Asian Studies*, 42 (1982): 63–90.

Murdock, George P. *Social Structure*. New York: Macmillan Co., 1949.

Myerhoff, Barbara G. *Number Our Days*. New York: Simon and Schuster, 1980.

Myerhoff, Barbara G., and Jay Ruby. "Introduction." In *A Crack in the Mirror*, edited by Jay Ruby, 1–35. Philadelphia: University of Pennsylvania Press, 1982.

Nam, Andrew C. *North Korea: Her Past, Reality, and Impression*. Kalamazoo: Center for Korean Studies, Western Michigan University, 1978.

Noble, Harold Joyce. *Embassy at War*. Seattle: University of Washington Press, 1975.

Nukunya, G. K. *Kinship and Marriage among the Anlo Ewe*. New York: Humanities Press, 1969.

Ohnuki-Tierney, Emiko. *Illness and Healing among the Sakhalin Ainu: A Symbolic Interpretation*. New York: Cambridge University Press, 1981.

————. *Illness and Culture in Contemporary Japan: An Anthropological View*. New York: Cambridge University Press, 1984.

————. " 'Native' Anthropologists." *American Ethnologist*, 11 (1984): 584–586.

Osgood, Cornelius. *The Koreans and Their Culture*. New York: Ronald Press, 1951.

Pak, Kyŏng-sik. *Chōsenjin kyoseirenkō no kiroku* (A record of involuntary Korean migration). Tokyo: Miraisha, 1965.

Pelto, Pertti J. *Anthropological Research: The Structure of Inquiry*. New York: Harper and Row, 1970.

Peterson, John H., Jr., Barbara G. Spencer, and Choong S. Kim. *Choctaw Demographic Survey*. Philadelphia, Miss.: Mississippi Band of Choctaw Indians, 1974.

Peterson, Mark. "Some Korean Attitudes Toward Adoption." *Korea Journal*, 17 (1977): 28–31.

Powdermaker, Hortense. *Stranger and Friend: The Way of an Anthropologist*. New York: W. W. Norton and Co., 1966.

Radcliffe-Brown, A. R., and D. Forde, eds. *African Systems of Kinship and Marriage*. New York: Oxford University Press, 1950.

Redfield, Margaret Park, ed. *Human Nature and The Study of Society: The Papers of Robert Redfield*. Vol. 1. Chicago: University of Chicago Press, 1962.

Rees, David. *Korea: The Limited War*. New York: St. Martin's Press, 1964.

Republic of Korea National Red Cross. *The Dispersed Families in Korea*. Seoul: Republic of Korea National Red Cross, 1977.

Richardson, Miles. "Anthropologist—The Myth Teller." *American Ethnologist*, 2 (1975): 517–533.

Riley, John W., and Wilbur Schramm. *The Reds Take a City: The Communist Occupation of Seoul, with Eyewitness Accounts*. New Brunswick, N.J.: Rutgers University Press, 1951.

Rosenblatt, Roger. *Children of War*. Garden City, N.Y.: Anchor Books, 1983.

Ruby, Jay, ed. *A Crack in the Mirror*. Philadelphia: University of Pennsylvania Press, 1982.

Rynkiewich, Michael A., and James P. Spradley, eds. *Ethics and Anthropology: Dilemmas in Fieldwork*. New York: John Wiley and Sons, 1976.

Sandusky, Michael C. *America's Parallel*. Alexandria, Va.: Old Dominion Press, 1983.

Sayles, Myrna. "Behind Locked Doors." In *Applied Anthropology in America*, edited by Elizabeth Eddy and William L. Partridge, 201–228. New York: Columbia University Press, 1978.

Scalapino, Robert A., and Chong-sik Lee. *Communism in Korea*. 2 pts. Berkeley: University of California Press, 1972.

Seekins, Donald M. "The Society and Its Environment." In *North Korea: A Country Study (Area Handbook Series)*, edited by Frederica M. Bunge, 47–105. Washington, D.C.: U.S. Government Printing Office, 1981.

Sorensen, Clark W. "Women, Men; Inside, Outside: The Division of Labor in Rural Central Korea." In *Korean Women: View from the Inner Room*, edited by Laurel Kendall and Mark Peterson, 63–78. New Haven: East Rock Press, 1983.

————. "Patterns of Misinformation in South Korean Fieldwork." Paper presented at the eighty-fourth annual meeting of the American Anthropological Association, Washington, D.C., December 4–8, 1985.

Spindler, George D. "An Anthropology of Education." *Council on Anthropology and Education Newsletter*, 4 (1973): 14–16.

Srinivas, M. N. *Social Change in Modern India*. Berkeley: University of California Press, 1966.

Steinberg, David I. "Development Lessons from the Korean Experience—A Review Article." *Journal of Asian Studies*, 42 (1982): 91–104.

Stone, I. F. *The Hidden History of the Korean War*. New York: Monthly Review Press, 1952.

Sturtevant, William C. "Studies in Ethnoscience." *American Anthropologist*, 66, pt. 2 (1964): 99–131.

Suh, Dae-sook. *The Korean Communist Movement, 1918–1948*. Princeton: Princeton University Press, 1967.

Sumner, William Graham. *Folkways*. New York: New American Library, 1959.

Tauber, Irene. *The Population of Japan*. Princeton: Princeton University Press, 1958.

Tieszen, Helen Rose. "Korean Proverbs about Women." In *Virtues in Conflict: Tradition and the Korean Woman Today*, edited by Sandra Mattielli, 49–66. Seoul: Royal Asiatic Society, Korean Branch, 1977.

Tocqueville, Alexis de. *Democracy in America*. Translated by Henry Reeve. 2 vols. New York: Co-operative Publication Society, 1900.

U.S. Department of the Army. *Korea—1950*. Washington, D.C.: U.S. Government Printing Office, 1952.

Veblen, Thorstein. *The Theory of the Leisure Class*. New York: Modern Library, 1934.

Vogel, Ezra F. "The Japanese Family." In *Comparative Family Systems*, edited by M. F. Nimkoff, 287–300. Boston: Houghton Mifflin Co., 1965.

Wagner, Edward W. *The Korean Minority in Japan: 1904–1950*. New York: Institute of Pacific Relations, 1951.

———. "The Korean Chokpo as a Historical Source." In *Studies on Asian Genealogy*, edited by S. J. Palmer, 141–252. Provo, Utah: Brigham Young University Press, 1971.

———. "Two Early Genealogies and Women's Status in Early Yi Dynasty Korea." In *Korean Women: View from the Inner Room*, edited by Laurel Kendall and Mark Peterson, 23–32. New Haven: East Rock Press, 1983.

Wallace, Anthony F. C. "Review of: *The Revolution in Anthropology* by I. C. Jarvie." *American Anthropologist*, 68 (1966): 1254–1255.

Whiting, Allen S. *China Crosses the Yalu: The Decision to Enter the Korean War*. Stanford: Stanford University Press, 1960.

Wilson, Monica. *Good Company: A Study of Nyakyusa Agevillages*. London: Oxford University Press, 1951.

Wolf, Arthur P., and Chieh-shan Haung. *Marriage and Adoption in China, 1845–1945*. Stanford: Stanford University Press, 1980.

Yang, Sung Chul. *Korea and Two Regimes: Kim Il Sung and Park Chung Hee*. Cambridge, Mass.: Schenkman Publishing Co., 1981.

———. "Socialist Education in North Korea." In *Journey to North Korea: Personal Perceptions*, edited by C. I. Eugene Kim and B. C. Koh. Research Papers and Policy Studies, no. 8, 63–83. Berkeley: Institute of East Asian Studies, 1983.

Yoshio, Abe. *Nihon shushigaku to Chōsen* (Japanese Neo-Confucianism and Korea). Tokyo: Tokyo University Press, 1965.

———. "Nihon jukyō no hatten to Yi T'oegye (The development of Confucianism in Japan and Yi T'oegye)." *Han*, 1 (1972): 3–27.

Index

Agnate, 41
Aguilar, John L., 12
Allied forces, 27
Ancestor worship, 39, 42, 63, 71, 86–87, 97, 131
Anticommunist law, 7, 143; abrogation of, 105
Anti-Japanese movement, 19, 69, 90
Armistice, Korean War, 98. *See also* Ceasefire
Association of the Families of Koreans in China, 108

Benedict, Ruth, 11

Cash, J. W., 46
Ceasefire, Korean War, 3, 64; negotiating, 35. *See also* Armistice
Central Asia. *See* Mail exchange
Central Committee of the North Korean Worker's Party (KWP), 104
Chastity, 44, 74; ethical standard of, 67; of widows, 56; of women, 56
Chientao, Manchuria, 19, 87; Korean independence fighters in, 19; Korean population in, 19
China: attitude toward family reunion,
21–22; conscripted soldiers sent to, 24; cultural heritage of Koreans in, 20–21; discrimination against Koreans in, 20; entry visa from, 23; ethnic heritage in, 20; influence on patterns of Korean kinship, 37; Korean provisional government in, 19; Koreans in, 18–22, 108
Chinese dynasties: Ch'ing, 18; invasion and domination by, 16; T'ang, 18; Yüan, 18
Chinese People's Volunteers (CPV), 20, 32–33, 80; invasion of, 81. *See also* Chinese troops
Chinese troops (soldiers), 34, 63, 82, 128. *See also* Chinese People's Volunteers (CPV)
Choi, Jai-seuk, 40
Ch'ongnyŏn, 25, 106, 108
Clans, 41–44, 46, 87, 93, 97
Class endogamy, 37
Cold War, 18, 20, 28
Committee for the Return of Displaced Civilians (CRDC), 99
Concubinage, 43, 48
Confucianism, 67, 71; classics of, 48; Confucianists, 87–89; ethics of, 52, 92; teachings of, 40; virtues of, 37, 90
Cuba. *See* Mail exchange

About the Author

Choong Soon Kim was born and reared in Korea. He witnessed firsthand the carnage of both World War II and the Korean War, and the dispersal of Korean families as a result of these wars. After fifteen years of residence and fieldwork in other cultures, he returned to Korea with the ability to look at Koreans and their culture from new perspectives. Kim received law degrees from Yonsei University, an M.A. from Emory University, and a Ph.D. from the University of Georgia. In 1981 he became professor and chairman of the department of sociology and anthropology at the University of Tennessee at Martin.